# Eagle Motifs IN America

## Decade art quilt series 1770 to the present

Susan E. Wildemuth

Schiffer Publishing Ltd
4880 Lower Valley Road • Atglen, PA 19310

Library of Congress Control Number: 2013954538



Designed by Matt Goodman

Type set in Handel, Book Antiqua, and Frutiger

ISBN: 978-0-7643-4527-2
Printed in China

Published by Schiffer Publishing, Ltd.
4880 Lower Valley Road
Atglen, PA 19310
Phone: (610) 593-1777; Fax: (610) 593-2002
E-mail: Info@schifferbooks.com

# Dedication

To my dad, husband, and son, who are my heroes, our beautiful daughter-in-law, granddaughter, and my mom for teaching me perseverance.

# Contents

# Acknowledgments


Before I thank anyone else, I need to thank Gaye Ingram and Melanie Bishop. Gaye Rice Ingram of Ruston, Louisiana, did her pre-publication editing magic and shared sage advice that helped make this good project better. Melanie Weis Bishop McCalley of Bettendorf, Iowa, and Best Days Photography, is the creative soul who produced many of the amazing photographs of the eagle motif quilts for this project.

The artists and historians who used their knowledge and needle work to tell the story of the eagle motif in American quilts are: Kate Adams; Karen Biedler Alexander; Ramona Bates, M.D.; Don Beld; Georgia Bonesteel; Linda Carlson; Connie Chunn; Grace J. Errea; Deborah Fell; Leigh Fellner; Bobbi Finley; Bernice Foster; Barbara Garrett; Gaye Rice Ingram; Sharon Malec; Susan Price Miller; Jennifer Tenney Myers; Teddy McMahon Pruett; Deborah S. Rake; Bets Ramsey; Kathie Ratcliffe; Lisa Ruetz; Sandra Starley; Terry Clothier Thompson; Greta VanDenBerg-Nestle; and Kimberly Wulfert, Ph.D.

A special thank you to my essay writers, Kimberly Wulfert, Ph.D., Bets Ramsey, Gaye Rice Ingram, Karen Biedler Alexander, and Betty Ross.

A special thank you goes to these organizations, and the people involved in them: Iowa Illinois Quilt Study Group; American Quilt Study Group; and Quilt History List, Kris Driessen, Moderator.

A special thank you to the staff at Schiffer Publishing, Jeff Snyder Lori Radun, Don Beld, Cindy Rennels, Randy Marshall, Barbara Vukits, and Luanne Evans.

I could not have envisioned or completed this work without the love and support of my husband, Keith, son, Brian, daughter-in-law, Nikki, and granddaughter, Audrina, who are my safe harbors in calm and choppy waters, and my mother and mother-in-law who taught me, through example, about strength, courage, and overcoming adversity. Their gifts are incalculable.

# Introduction

"Houston, Tranquility Base here. The *Eagle* has landed."

—**Neil Armstrong**, *Apollo 11 Space Mission, 1969*

*The Eagle Has Landed*, 2005. Cotton, quilt pieced by Chrys Day and Christine Anning, and machine quilted by Chrys Day, 69" x 89". Collection of Author. *Photograph by Best Days Photography.*

American Bald Eagles. Detroit Zoo. *Photograph by Barbara Vukits.*

## Eagles: The Symbols of Our Nation

Come to the Mississippi River region, where Iowa meets Illinois, in January and you will see them. Majestic and regal, they touch something very deep in our souls and rouse patriotic feelings of honor, duty, and love of country. What is this amazing creature that brings out such strong emotions in us? It is the symbol of our nation: the American Bald Eagle.

# Eagle Motifs in Quilts: Pinpointing the Inspiration

Material historians can point to no one source and say, "Here is where the original inspiration for the eagle motifs found in American quilts." The use of the eagle is found everywhere in the material life of Americans from the eighteenth century onward. From the earliest days of our republic, any woman wanting to find an image she might adapt to the needle and home arts has had a wide range of sources. Those adaptable image sources include:

**1.** Immigrants who brought their love of the eagle motif with them when they crossed the ocean from Europe and settled in America.
**2.** Native Americans, for whom the eagle was a powerful and ubiquitous symbol.
**3.** Federal materials that employ the American Bald Eagle as the symbol of the United States and American patriotism.
**4.** Advertising and documents of the Republican party.
**5.** Advertising signs found in the materials of taverns, inns, businesses, organizations, and popular print;
**6.** Figureheads on flags, ships, buildings.
**7.** National coinage.
**8.** The work of wood carvers and folk-artists like Wilhelm Schimmel (1817 to 1890), a German-born wood carver famous for his "fat bellied" spread-winged eagle carvings, some smooth and some crosshatched; Schimmel used his carvings to obtain food and shelter. His eagles are very similar to the eagle motif that appeared on the eagle on the diagonal quilts associated with Pennsylvania during the nineteenth and twentieth centuries.
**9.** The Great Seal of the United States.
**10.** Materials of our government—including materials used by the armed forces: badges and medals—programs and departments of the federal government.
**11.** Woven coverlets from eighteenth and nineteenth century America.
**12.** The work and materials produced by bird and wildlife enthusiasts.
**13.** Decorative and commemorative household items.
**14.** The work of furniture makers (inlay eagles on furniture from the Federal period).
**15.** Materials and textiles associated with wars, elections, military service, or national crisis and national history commemorations.

Walter Carlin "Babe" Parks.
*Photograph Courtesy of Betty Parks.*

# Collecting Eagle Quilts

I collect antique, vintage, and new eagle quilts, not the wildlife variety, but the patriotic version because they remind me of my favorite teacher. He was a salesman by occupation, but a teacher by heart. He taught me how to ride a bike, make pie crusts from scratch with his "secret" ingredient, and how to keep between the white lines on highways with a 1960s Rambler. He also taught me there were good men in the world who treated women with dignity and respect. My father was both a gentle man and gentleman. He provided the template by which I chose a husband and raised a son.

Growing up in Melrose, Iowa, my father dreamed of becoming an aviation engineer. After high school, he wanted to enroll in college; but, as it did for so many others of his generation, Pearl Harbor changed his life plan. Dad enlisted in the United States Navy and was sent to the Pacific on the *St. Lo*, where he served as an Aviation Machinist Mate. Somewhere off the Philippine Islands, the *St. Lo* was hit by a Kamikaze, and someone gave the order to abandon ship. Dad went over the side with only one shoe and his billfold, in which he had tucked a Sacred Heart Badge his mother had given him when he went overseas. His mother's goal with that badge was to give her son a piece of home to carry in his pocket. The heart is a symbol of love and faith from a mother who knows her son is about to embark on a journey that will change his life.

Sacred Heart Badge, c. 1976, Assumption Catholic High School, Davenport, Iowa, Graduation Gift. Sacred Heart Badges, rosary beads, St. Anthony Medals, or St. Christopher Medals are traditional first communion, confirmation, or graduation gifts in the author's Irish Catholic family, usually given by a grandparent, aunt/uncle, sibling, or parent to the honoree. Collection of Susan Wildemuth. *Photograph by Susan Wildemuth.*

The Fourth of July was one of my dad's favorite holidays. Every year, Mom and Dad took me and my brothers to the town celebration on the square. Hands down, the fireworks were the highlight of the day, but the parade after lunch was something to be seen too. Our father made sure we understood and observed parade etiquette from our earliest years. When the honor or color guard walked by, men and women who served in the military, stood up as one and put hands on hearts. It was, Dad told us, a sign of respect and a way to say thank you for their service.

I can pull up memories of WWI veterans marching in our town parade. These thin, work worn men seemed to grow taller when they carried the American Flag. One of us kids always asked Dad if he'd ever seen a Civil War veteran march in a parade. "When I was a little boy," he'd say, and then we would get a history lesson to match the question. None of us minded, for dad could tell a story everyone wanted to hear. I think my father's one regret was that he never got that college education he had planned, but he was an avid reader. To the little girl he used to take on Saturday morning soda fountain dates, he was the smartest man in the world.

When my dad passed away, my mother asked each of us children, "Is there something you would like that belonged to your dad?"

I knew exactly what I wanted. I asked Mom for his Sacred Heart Badge, the one he had when he went over the side of his ship. Some sixty plus years later, the badge has a home in my son's billfold, a gift from a mother to a son the fall he left for college. His mother's goal with that badge is to give her son a piece of home to carry in his pocket, a heart, a symbol of love and faith from a mother who knows her son is about to embark on a journey that will change his life. Brian, my son, was three years old when my father passed away, but Dad would be so proud of the gentle man and gentleman his grandson turned out to be.

**—Susan E. Wildemuth**, *The Babe's Eaglet*

# Project Overview
# The Inspiration for the Project

I collect eagle quilts, and I wanted to include in my collection some of the historic quilts containing eagle motifs. I knew I was probably never going to find, outside of a museum setting, an actual 1930s NRA Blue Eagle quilt or an original Emma S. Tyrell *Lone Eagle* quilt honoring Charles Lindbergh's flight. I also wanted to add others like these to my collection so I might assemble and share a representative history of the eagle motifs used in American quiltmaking, decade by decade.

What to do?

On one of my daily walks, an idea occurred to me: I might commission miniature quilts or studio art pieces by quilt artists and historians whose work I admired. Thereby, I would be able to create a coherent, decade-by-decade group of quilts that traced the use of the eagle motif in American quiltmaking. Such a collection would have significance of its own, as contemporary reflections of this honored tradition. And it will also help fill in blank spots in my existing collection of eagle quilts.

The more I thought about this idea, the more I liked it. The bonus to such a project was that it would include the work of some of the best studio quilt artists or quilt historians of the twenty-first century.

I took a chance and approached my first quilt artist, designer, and historian, and that dear soul said yes.

The rest is now history.

# The Plan

Each maker would select a decade in America's history to represent in a quilt format. The finished quilt could be no larger than 24 inches in width and length. Beyond those general considerations were the following:

1. An eagle motif had to be incorporated into the piece.
2. The piece might be based on the artist's interpretation of an antique eagle quilt or might be an entirely original design.
3. Either by eagle motif, fabric, design, or story told, the quilt had to represent the decade chosen by its maker.
4. Each quilted piece needed to be signed, dated, and named, with a sleeve for hanging.
5. Each piece might be hand pieced and quilted, machine pieced and quilted, or a combination of both techniques might be employed. *And ...*
6. Modern, period, or reproduction fabrics might be used.

# Series
# Artists and Stories

"Methinks it is a token of healthy and gentle characteristics, when women (and men) of high thoughts and accomplishment love to sew; especially as they are never more at home in their own hearts than while so occupied."

—Nathaniel Hawthorne, *The Marble Faun*, 1859

*A New Nation*, 1770 to 1779, 22.5" x 22", Terry Clothier Thompson, Kansas. Collection of Author.
*Photograph by Best Days Photography.*

# A New Nation

Terry Clothier Thompson was the first one to tackle the eighteenth century: she chose the 1770s. If you have seen—or own—her book *Made in America 1776 to 1830: Quilts of the Daughters of Liberty*, you will know that this time period of American history is one of her favorites.

The inspiration for her piece was an image of the Daughter of Liberty. To represent a new nation, Terry added the design of a baby eagle. Next, she appliquéd her Daughter of Liberty and baby eagle on a fabric reproduced from of the design by an American textile printer in the Revolutionary War era. The embroidery embellishments add interest and dimension to the piece that honors and celebrates the birth of our nation.

**Quilt Technique:** Appliqué with some hand quilting, machine piecing and quilting, and embroidery.

Detail, *A New Nation*, Kansas. Daughter of Liberty and eagle view. Collection of Author. *Photograph by Best Days Photography.*

9

# Terry Clothier Thompson

Terry Clothier Thompson, Kansas. *Submitted.*

"My interest in quilts began in the 1960s, with my desire to create household textiles by hand," Terry Clothier Thompson writes. "Although my grandmother had encouraged me to embroider at the age of nine, I showed no interest in quilts until years later, when I was a young mother of two children. Women's magazines of that time featured articles on needlework, crochet, knitting, and quilt making and my thoughts turned to quiltmaking. This interest led me into an art that has fascinated me for forty years."

Terry began collecting and studying nineteenth century quilts, teaching classes for beginning quilt makers, and designing patterns for her classes. In 1973, along with three friends, she opened one of the first quilt shops in the Midwest, the Quilting Bee, where she bought and sold vintage quilts and clothing and taught classes in quiltmaking. After eleven years of retail, she left the shop, hitting the road to teach and lecture at quilt guilds all over the United States. "During this time I began to write books about quiltmaking and to tell stories of my pioneering Clothier family. Interviewing my aunts and mother, I had learned how the women in my family coped with the Civil War, World War I, and World War II, and their stories found their way into my writing and work."

Terry is a quilt artist, writer, historian, pattern designer, and fabric designer for Moda fabrics. She served as one of the principal documenters for the Kansas Quilt Project, and the resulting book, *Kansas Quilts and Quilters* (University Press of Kansas), includes her chapter on conversation prints. Terry presents programs and workshops featuring her books: *Made in America by the Daughters of Liberty: 1776 to 1830; Prairie Quilts & Pioneer Stories; Quilts & Stories from the Peace Creek Homestead*; and, most recently, *The People of the Plains*. She also teaches a three-day class in her studio called FabriCamp, where quilt historians, appraisers, and artists learn to date their antique and vintage quilts.

**Website:** www.terrythompson.com

*A Salute to the Founding of a Nation*, 1780 to 1789, 24.5" x 24.25", Karen Biedler Alexander, Washington. Collection of Author. *Photograph by Best Days Photography.*

# A Salute to the Founding of a Nation

I began this project by researching the history of eagle images popular in American history over the past 200-plus years. Then I looked for reproduction fabrics that reflected the 1780s, the decade I had chosen for my contribution to this collection. I knew George Washington fabric was available, and I also knew there was a fabric with early eagle images.

Once the fabric arrived, I cut out several different images and began to play with their placement. I ended up with three possible choices for layouts, and I photographed them. I auditioned some possible border fabrics and determined what size each border needed to be so the quilt would fit within the required size and would look balanced. Then I selected one of the three layouts I had photographed and began basting. I was ready to begin the appliqué process, and the hours I spent doing the Broderie Perse was a pure joy. Dream Cotton was my choice of batting.

I even found doing the back of this quilt fun! I decided to attach one page of a timeline from 1780 to the back of the quilt. The next morning I decided to add a pocket instead of a label. The pocket gave me the opportunity to print a photo and bio, again on fabric, which I then folded and stuck in the label pocket.

*– Karen Biedler Alexander*

**Quilt Technique:** Appliqué, embroidery, and hand piecing and quilting.

Detail, *A Salute to the Founding of a Nation*, Washington. Broderie Perse, eagle. Collection of Author. *Photograph by Susan Wildemuth.*

# Karen Biedler Alexander

Karen Biedler Alexander, Washington. *Submitted. Photography by Steve Horn Photography.*

Karen Biedler Alexander grew up in northeastern Ohio and lived abroad for two separate periods in her childhood. Yet her roots and sense of home lie in the Shenandoah Valley of Virginia, where her Swiss ancestor first settled in 1740. Living with her husband and children in Virginia from 1979 to 1983, Karen learned to quilt. She also joined the American Quilt Study Group, thereby beginning a lifelong study of history as it is found in quilts, textiles, quilting practices, and quilters' stories. Karen has been active in quilt guilds wherever she has lived, even in periods when she was primarily studying history, not making quilts. Her first article on the subject of quilts was published in 1983.

As her children entered high school, Karen also became a Meeting Planner,working professionally in a field where she had volunteered since her college days.

In the late 1990s, Karen became active in the work of The Quilters Hall of Fame. In 2004, on the occasion of the group's 25th anniversary, she co-chaired the Grand Opening of the organization's new home, the historic Marie Webster House in Marion, Indiana. In 2005, she became the second president of The Quilters Hall of Fame. Karen currently works as a member of the Signature Quilt Pilot Project Team of The Quilt Index, a division of The Alliance for American Quilts. She also serves on the board of her local historical society on Lopez Island, Washington, and is an advisor to the newly formed Oregon Quilt Project, in addition to writing three quilt history blogs. She continues the lectures on quilt history that she has presented since the late 1990s.

**Blogs:** *Quilt History Reports.* karenquilt.blogspot.com/,
*Enchanted Quilters of Lopez Island.* enchantedquiltersoflopezisland.blogspot.com
*Honorees of The Quilters Hall of Fame.* honoreesofthequiltershalloffame.blogspot.com

# The Great Seal

## Kimberly Wulfert, Ph.D.

*Great Seal of the United States Eagle Quilt,* Pennsylvania, c. 1940. Cotton (87" x 106"). Parks Wildemuth Collection. *Photograph by Best Days Photography.*

*Kimberly Wulfert, Ph.D., California. Submitted. Photograph by Caitlin Jean Petersen.*

The eagle on the first Great Seal of the United States in 1782 looked quite different than it does today. The American Bald Eagle, symbolizing supreme power and authority, was not the first eagle chosen for the Seal.

The idea to design an official engraved seal for the United States of America, as done in England and Europe, surfaced at the conclusion of the Continental Congress and writing of the Declaration of Independence meeting in July 1776.

The Congress envisioned the Great Seal as a symbol, a sort of coat of arms representing the newly declared country. Benjamin Franklin, Thomas Jefferson, and John Adams were the first three members of a committee appointed to deliver a Great Seal and device for the seal. No one thought it would take six years and many images drafted to produce a seal everyone could agree represented the thirteen colonies as one in their sovereignty, with equal ranking to other countries.

The eagle was not part of the first seals that were suggested, largely because a European style coat of arms was their point of reference. When the eagle did appear in a 1780 drafting, it was a small, crested Imperial White Eagle with scrawny L shaped legs and no neck. They were indecisive about showing the wings down as if in flight or wing tips up and open wide. The Congress was

Detail, *Great Seal of the United States Eagle Quilt*, appliqué and embroidered center medallion depicting a variation of the Great Seal (eagle view). Parks Wildemuth Collection. *Photograph by Best Days Photography.*

*Great Seal of the United States. Crewel embroidery kit. Parks Wildemuth Collection. Photograph by Susan Wildemuth.*

still not satisfied and, so, decided to hand over all of the design ideas thus far to Charles Thomson, the Secretary of Congress.

We have Thomson to thank for deciding that the Native American bald eagle would prominently decorate the face of the seal and for placing a bundle of arrows in the left talon, a fruitless olive branch in the right one, and placing the already established motto, *E Pluribus Unum* ("out of many, one"), on a scroll held by the eagle's beak. The shield of stripes and a chief, hung without support upon the eagle's breast, symbolizing that the United States should rely on her own virtues.

The first seal was made of brass and came into being sometime between June and September 1782. Later Seals were made of steel. Design details were changed as an engraving wore out and had to be replaced. The Eagle grew noticeably stronger as the country gained strength.

In 1885, Tiffany and Company made the greatest changes to the eagle, forming the image in use today. The eagle's legs became muscular, with its larger, stronger talons holding the arrows and branch from behind, and an upper body appeared above the shield where white head and dark body feathers could be distinguished because of their masterful engraving.

Never lacking in symbolism, the olive branch with thirteen leaves noted the power of peace and the thirteen arrows, war. The eagle on the Seal always faced to its own right and peace. On the President's Seal, the eagle's head always faced toward the arrows on its left until President Truman, in 1945, ordered the eagle's head be turned toward the olive branch.

The last changes to the eagle's design were made in the 1904 steel die, the master of which we still use today. In this design, the eagle feathers became more pointed and the talon's joints were sharpened.

*– Kimberly Wulfert, Ph.D., California*

*1790s Eagle*, 1790 to 1799, 20.5" x 20.5", Ramona Bates, M.D., Arkansas. Collection of Author. *Photograph by Susan Wildemuth.*

# 1790s Eagle

Before accepting this commission, I pulled out some of my quilt books to investigate the appearance of quilts during the 1790 to 1799 period. I wanted to be sure I could deliver a quilt that looked like it might have come from the 1790s.

In *Clues in the Calico* (1989), Barbara Brackman observes that in the mid-eighteenth century most quilted work was done on whole cloth. "Like bed quilts," Brackman writes, "petticoats were of whole cloth, often silk or glazed wool, quilted with designs such as feathers and flowers." (pp.14–15)

In *The American Quilt* (1994), Roderick Kiracofe agrees, stating, "Many quilts from this period tend to be of the 'whole cloth' style, made from a length of fabric that had not been pieced into a design." (pp. 46–48)

Thus, Sue Wildemuth and I decided mine should be a whole cloth quilt. I purchased white glazed cotton online and, while I waited for it to arrive, I began the design process. I was surprised to find very few examples from this period in my quilting books. My husband, however, had a perfect source, *The Eagle on U.S. Firearms* by John W. Jordan. During this time period, I learned, eagles had down-turned wings and long, turkey-like necks. *The Woman's Day Book of American Needlework* by Rose Wilder Lane provided a beautiful example of just such an eagle in a counterpane from the Henry Ford Museum. The original design was embroidered, but I knew I could make it work as a quilting design. I simply needed to reconfigure the wings so they bent down and then turn the oval into a circle.

Once I had completed my design and transferred it onto the fabric, I began the process of hand quilting the piece I named *1790s Eagle*.

– *Ramona Bates, M.D.*

**Quilt Technique**: Hand quilting.

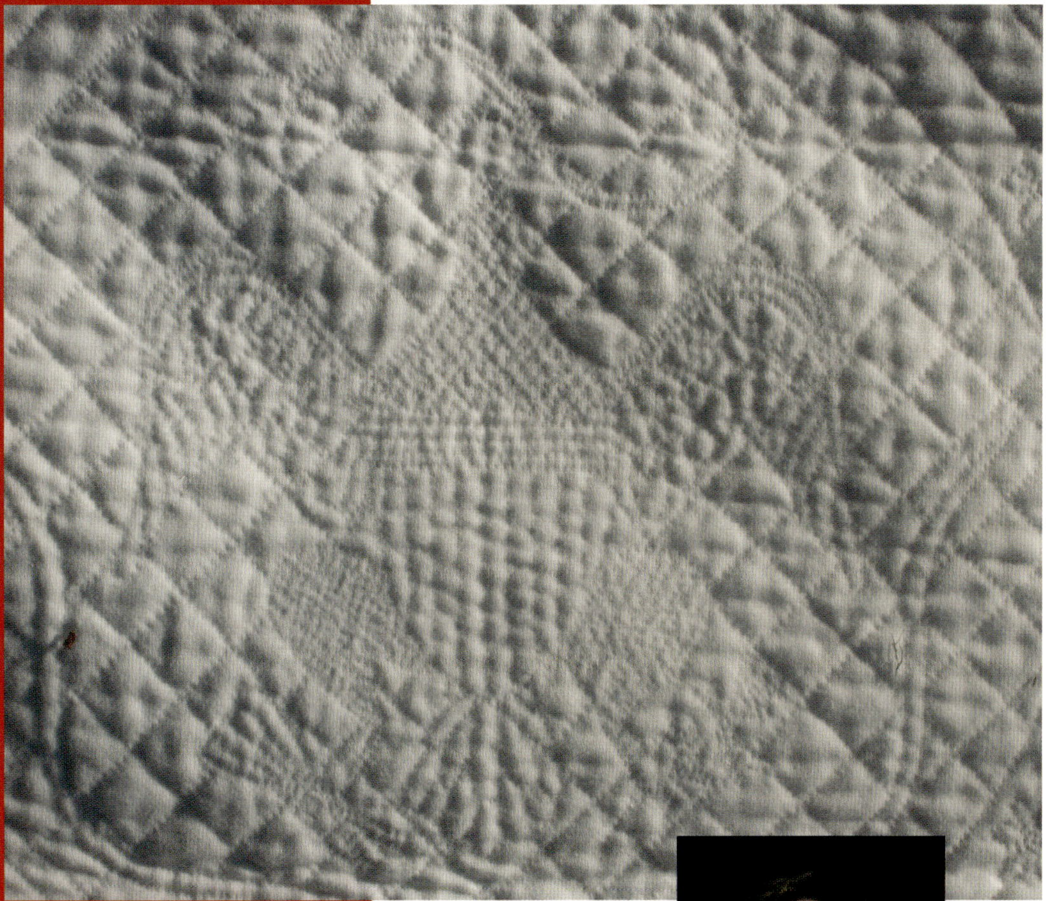

Detail, *1790s Eagle*, Arkansas. Eagle close-up. Collection of Author. *Photograph Courtesy of Ramona Bates, M.D.*

# Ramona Bates, M.D.

Ramona Bates, M.D., Arkansas. *Submitted.*

Dr. Ramona Bates, a plastic surgeon, grew up sewing in central Arkansas. She says, "My mother, who taught me to sew, used to say I began begging for needle and thread when I was only five years old. My love of quilts and quiltmaking comes from my paternal grandmother, and I am lucky to have two of her quilt tops, which my mother quilted for me."

Ramona began making quilts in her teens. She says, "Even though I made my first quilt when I was sixteen years old and made a few baby quilts through the years, I really began quilting seriously in 1990, when I opened my solo plastic surgery office. I needed a distraction while the office was slow, and I also wanted some quilts to go on the office walls."

Ramona adds that she is "mostly self taught through books, magazines, and quilting shows aired on my local Public Broadcasting television channel. I have entered quilt contests over the years as a way to challenge myself."

In 2000, she won a First and a Second Place Award for two miniature quilts in the annual quilt show of the Arkansas Quilters Guild. In 2007 her quilt *Will the Circle Be Unbroken* won the award for Best Hand Quilting in the Great Arkansas Quilt Show, hosted by the Historic Arkansas Museum.

**Blog:** *Suture for a Living.* rlbatesmd.blogspot.com

*Washington's Eagle*, 1790 to 1799, 24.5" x 24.5", Greta VanDenBerg-Nestle, Pennsylvania. Collection of Author. *Photograph by Susan Wildemuth.*

# Washington's Eagle

Early whole cloth quilts have always been a favorite of mine, especially those made of woven wools and silks. As a machine quilter, I seek inspiration from the beautiful and often dense quilting found in those early quilts. In recent years I have also explored the process of spinning, dyeing, and weaving fibers available to early American quilters. When Sue Wildemuth presented me the opportunity to make a quilt representing the 1790s, I knew my quilt would have to be a whole cloth quilt, constructed of hand- dyed wool and silk, and that it would be machine quilted with very fine silk thread.

I also knew the eagle I wanted to feature would have to be a quilted version of the majestic bird that appears on inaugural buttons and coins that honor George Washington, the first President of the United States elected under The Constitution that became the law of the land on March 4, 1789. While numerous events during the last decade of the eighteenth century helped shape our government, the most important precedent was the thoughtful and cautious manner by which George Washington acted as President in areas where the new Constitution was unclear. His wisdom lives on in his "Farewell Address," written when he left office in 1796, still considered one of the most important documents in America's history.

– *Greta VanDenBerg-Nestle*

**Quilt Technique:** Machine quilting and hand-dyed wool.

Detail, *Washington's Eagle,* Pennsylvania. Eagle view Back. Collection of Author. *Photograph by Susan Wildemuth.*

Detail, *Washington's Eagle,* Pennsylvania. Eagle view Front on wool. Collection of Author. *Photograph by Susan Wildemuth.*

# Greta VanDenBerg-Nestle

Greta VanDenBerg-Nestle, Pennsylvania. *Submitted.*

An antique doll quilt made by her maternal great grandmother inspired Greta VanDenBerg-Nestle to make her first quilt when she was nine years old. That quilt marked the beginning of her research into antique quilts and sewing machines. It was also the start of her collection of antique textiles. The daughter of a mechanical engineer and an artist, she continues to enjoy the blend of precision and creativity available to her in the design and construction of quilts. She and her husband have three daughters, two granddaughters, and a grandson. She is a quilt artist and a member of the American Quilt Study Group.

**Blog:** *Splinters en Threads*
splintersenthreads.blogspot.com/

# 1800 to 1809

*E Pluribus Unum,* 1800 to 1809, 20.5" x 21.5", Bets Ramsey, Tennessee. Collection of Author. *Photograph by Susan Wildemuth.*

## E Pluribus Unum

When researching an eagle motif for her 1800s piece, Southern quilt historian, author, and textile artist Bets Ramsey turned for inspiration to her beloved state of Tennessee and a quilt created by one of its early quilt makers. Inscribed "Rebecah Foster, Nashville, October 5, 1808," this masterpiece can be found in the collection of the Tennessee State Museum (Nashville, Tennessee) and was featured in two photographic plates in the 1992 edition of the book *Quilts of America* by Patsy and Myron Orlofsky (p. 195).

Bets redrafted the eagle design from the Foster quilt and created a masterpiece of her own, which she calls *E Pluribus Unum.*

**Quilt Technique:** Appliqué, hand piecing and quilting, and embroidery.

Detail, *E Pluribus Unum*, Tennessee. Eagle view. Collection of Author. *Photograph by Susan Wildemuth.*

Bets Ramsey, Tennessee. *Submitted.*

## Bets Ramsey

Bets Ramsey entered the world of quiltmaking and its history in 1971. She has taught, lectured, and written about quilts ever since. In 1984, she and Merikay Waldvogel began a survey of Tennessee quilts that resulted in the book *The Quilts of Tennessee*, published in 1986, and a touring exhibition of quilts featured in this book.

For seventeen years, her Southern Quilt Symposium at the Hunter Museum of American Art in Chattanooga attracted participants from coast to coast and made a major contribution to the quilt revival of the twentieth century. Her book, *Southern Quilts: Surviving Relics of the Civil War,* coauthored with Merikay Waldvogel, was published in 1998.

She is an award-winning exhibiting artist. Her work was included in the exhibition "The Art of Tennessee" at the Frist Center for the Visual Arts in Nashville, Tennessee. In 2003, a forty-two-year retrospective exhibition of her fiber works appeared in the Carroll Reece Museum of East Tennessee State University and the Leu Art Gallery of Belmont University.

Ramsey was inducted into the Quilters Hall of Fame in 2005. In 2008, the Alliance for American Quilts produced a biographical video about her career for its website. The following year, Bets received the Tennessee Governor's Award in the Arts for her work as artist, author, curator, and teacher.

*1810s Eagle,* 1810 to 1819, 9.25" x 8.25", Kathie Ratcliffe, Virginia. Collection of Author. *Photograph by Best Days Photography.*

# 1810s Eagle

Virginia quilt artist, historian, and collector Kathie Ratcliffe says her "challenge and joy is to use the inspiration of a favorite antique quilt and attempt to capture its essence in very small pieces," known in quilt circles as miniatures.

Kathie chose the 1810s for the quilt she would make and began researching quilts made in that decade that included eagle motifs. She found her inspiration in a quilt that makes its home in Vermont at the Shelburne Museum. A history enthusiast, she took on the challenge of reproducing the U.S. Navy quilt in the museum's permanent collection and featured in a photograph in the 1986 edition *All Flags Flying: American Patriotic Quilts as Expressions of Liberty* by Robert Bishop and Carter Houck (p. 12).

Kathie's attention to details, right down to the "four-poster" cut-out corners and embroidery embellishments, make this miniature quilt a masterpiece.

**Quilt Technique:** Machine piecing with hand sewing and embroidery.

Detail, *1810s Eagle*, Virginia. Eagle view. Collection of Author. *Photograph by Best Days Photography.*

Kathie Ratcliffe, Virginia. *Submitted.*

## Kathie Ratcliffe

Kathie Ratcliffe lives and works at the Nine Patch Studio in the National Historic Landmark village of Waterford, Virginia. A quilt artist and collector of antique quilts for thirty-five years, Kathie combines her needlework skills with her passion for nineteenth century pieced quilts. Her work reflects the progression in palette and design of quiltmakers in a dynamic century in American quilt art.

Using her growing knowledge of antique quilts and textiles, Kathie began piecing quilts at miniature scale, each one inspired by a quilt from the nineteenth century. This new direction gave her the opportunity to make quilts in distinctive regional genres and to document nineteenth century trends in fabrics and design styles, using the same vibrant colors and patterns that made the originals so exceptional. With the designs and colors of antique quilts in miniature scale, these warm and joyful works of art can grace walls and preserve the richness of America's quilt heritage.

Kathie's continuing challenge and joy is to use the inspiration of a favorite antique quilt and capture its essence in very small pieces. Her miniature quilts have appeared in the finest Americana shows and are in private collections nationally and abroad. She has been honored as one of the foremost traditional American textile artists and selected by museum professionals for inclusion in the *Directory of Traditional American Crafts of the magazine Early American Life.*

**Website:** *Nine Patch Studio.* www.ninepatchstudio.com/

*Anna's Eagle*, 1820 to 1829, 24" x 23.5", Bobbi Finley, California. Collection of Author. *Photograph by Best Days Photography.*

# Anna's Eagle

Bobbi Finley chose the 1820s as the decade she would represent in her quilt for this collection. She turned to the Daughters of the American Revolution Museum in Washington, D.C., to begin her eagle motif research. Studying the institution's magnificent early American quilts housed in their permanent collection, she chose the Anna Markey Garnhart Quilt as the inspiration for her piece.

The March/April 2005 issue of the DAR National Society's *American Spirit Magazine* article affords insight into Anna Garnhart's quiltmaking career:

> *From 1815 to 1830, Anna Garnhart made 11 quilts for each of her grandchildren. All feature extensive use of reverse appliqué. In this complex technique, the colored fabrics are slipped underneath the ground fabric, which is cut away in the desired shape, tucked under and stitched down to reveal and frame the colored fabric. The central motif in the nine surviving Garnhart quilts is either an eagle or fruit basket. One inspiration for her designs was her transfer ware pitcher commemorating the death of George Washington, which pictured the eagle of the Great Seal.*

Using Anna's eagle as inspiration, Bobbi drafted an eagle motif for her quilt, adding her own creative touches. Attention to detail, like the direction the eagle's head faced, the selection of fabric colors, and finely crafted cross hatch quilting makes this quilt a wonderful work of art.

**Quilt Technique:** Appliqué, hand quilting, and piecing.

Detail, *Anna's Eagle*, California. Eagle view. Collection of Author. *Photograph by Best Days Photography.*

## Bobbi Finley

Bobbi Finley, California. *Submitted. Photograph by Deb Rowden.*

Bobbi Finley makes prize winning quilts. She has a quilt in the collection of the American Museum of Folk Art in New York City. She has exhibited her work at the International Quilt Festival in Houston, Texas, and the American Quilter's Society Museum in Paducah, Kentucky. Her love of exploring the history of quilts and their makers has led her to participate actively in the American Quilt Study Group, where she has served as a board member and cocurator of special study-quilt exhibits. After living for a time in Williamsburg, Virginia, Bobbi now resides in her native state, California, with her cat, Thomas.

**Blog:** *Bobbi Finley: One Quilter's Journey.*
bobbifinleytilequilts.blogspot.com

*Birds of a Feather Fly Together,* 1830 to 1839, 24" x 23.25", Sandra Starley, Utah. Collection of Author. *Photograph by Best Days Photography.*

# Birds of a Feather Fly Together

"Birds of a Feather Fly Together" is my first commissioned piece, though I have been making quilts for national challenges for over a decade. I chose the 1830s, one of my favorite quilt eras, and after much research into early eagle quilts, I decided to adapt a bird quilt from my antique collection rather than reproducing an existing antique eagle quilt. I was inspired by a flying geese strippy quilt (c. 1830) with pheasant and duck toile. An English company, Talwin and Foster, printed the original circa 1800s blue and white toile. Luckily, I was able to find the perfect small-scale eagle print in a contemporary reproduction fabric, and I resized the flying geese down to a petite 1.5 x 3 inches to match those in my inspiration piece.

I did not try to follow the fabrics in the antique quilt exactly because I wanted to use a bit of my reproduction fabric collection. Nevertheless, I think I captured the feel of the original. I especially enjoyed the idea of the combination of bird themes, flying geese pattern, and eagle fabric. Hence the title, "Birds of a Feather Fly Together." I also liked the way the maker had joined the geese in pairs, so I followed her example: each pair of geese has its own set of fabrics.

**Quilt Technique:** Hand piecing and quilting and some machine work.

Detail, *Birds of a Feather Fly Together,* Utah. Antique c. 1830 flying geese with bird pheasant toile from Sandra Starley's personal collection is shown in a side-by-side comparison with her 1830s reproduction piece. The bird toile print in the original was printed c. 1775 to 1785 and is from an English company, Talwin and Foster. 1830s toile quilt from the Starley Antique Collection. *Photograph by Sandra Starley.*

Detail, *Birds of a Feather Fly Together,* Utah. Eagle view. Collection of Author. *Photograph by Best Days Photography.*

# Sandra Starley

Sandra Starley, Utah. *Submitted.*

Attorney Sandra Starley is one of the fewer than 100 nationally certified quilt appraisers in the United States. She is also a historian, researcher, quilt collector, lecturer, designer, and an instructor in quiltmaking. Active in the American Quilt Study Group and the Alliance for American Quilts, Sandra presents trunk shows on quilt history, fabric dating, on antique quilts as material culture, and teaching history one quilt at a time.

Sandra not only studies antique quilts, but she also enjoys reproducing quilts from her collection, especially in a small or miniature scale. She has won national awards both for her antique reproductions and her art quilts. Her work has been part of several traveling exhibits.

Blogs: *Quilt Art Star.* starleyquilts.blogspot.com/
*Textile Time Travels.* utahquiltappraiser.blogspot.com/

*From Sea to Shining Sea*, 1840 to 1849, 23" x 23", Gaye Rice Ingram, Louisiana. Collection of Author. *Photograph by Best Days Photography.*

# From Sea to Shining Sea

A decade of exuberant territorial expansion in the United States was experienced in the 1840s. The Louisiana Purchase had doubled the size of the nation in 1803, extending its western border beyond the Mississippi River to the current states of Montana and North Dakota and giving settlers west of the Appalachians access to the port of New Orleans and international trade. The War of 1812 and related wars with the southeastern Indians had pacified Alabama and southern Georgia and added east and west Florida to the nation.

By the 1820s, hordes of new settlers were moving into these lands, drawn by the rich soil, abundant rainfall, and long growing seasons required for growing cotton. Diarists describe roads filled day and night with covered wagons, barnyard animals, horses, and men on foot. By the late 1830s Texas, which stretched into southern Wyoming and included parts of Colorado and New Mexico, beckoned. By the end of the 1840s, treaties and the Mexican War moved the national border to the Pacific Ocean.

I chose to represent this expansive era in the name of my quilt, *From Sea to Shining Sea*. I envisioned what my great-great grandmothers, parts of this migration south and west, might have created, given the invitation I received. They were plain women whose families had moved from Virginia into the Mississippi Territory and set up small farms and timber operations. Living in a time of great hope and a land of strong sunshine, they would have chosen bright colors. Familiar with the older medallion format, as well as the block format that appears in the forties, they probably would have combined the two to create a quilt that, through design, symbolism, and fabric choices, reflected the exuberance of their era.

Accordingly, the central appliqué block of my quilt uses an eagle design common to public print at the time. The great bird is in flight, facing west, toward the Pacific Ocean, bearing the American flag with the old Liberty Cap of the Revolutionary years atop its staff. In his beak he holds the newly popular shield and ceremonial ribbons bearing the cry of the 1840s *Manifest Destiny*. Bouquets assembled from chintz and applied in overcast appliqué technique suggest the persistence of older preferences and techniques.

This block centers a pieced eight point star made from a reproduction rainbow print. Its background is reproduction chintz. A deep blue print border carries out the theme of the quilt. In the style of the decade, the quilting is on the diagonal except for the border, where I used the laurel leaf design, a motif also popular in this period.

In making this quilt, I honor Mary Elizabeth Mathes Jordan and Oleta Williams Rice, my maternal great grandmother and my mother, whose love of beauty and the home arts gave birth to my own.

*– Gaye Rice Ingram*

**Quilt Technique:** Appliqué, hand piecing, and quilting.

# Gaye Rice Ingram

Detail, *From Sea to Shining Sea*, Louisiana. Eagle view. Collection of Author. *Photograph by Susan Wildemuth.*

Gaye Rice Ingram grew up in Rapides Parish, Louisiana, in a home where quilts were owned, admired, and passed down. "Despite the books on quiltmaking that line my bookshelves and the quilts I have collected through purchase," she says, "I remain a traditional quiltmaker. I've never taken a class or treated my quilts as anything but parts of homemaking, ways of creating a home enriched by beauty."

One of her earliest memories is of falling asleep fingering French knots in the center of a Sunflower quilt her paternal grandmother had made. When she was six, her mother helped her make a four patch doll quilt. She began her first full-size quilt when she was a doctoral student in English at the University of Georgia in the 1960s. Seven years later she finished that quilt in time for the birth of her first child and went on to make more quilts for her home, always in patterns traditional in her family.

As professional work and family responsibilities claim more of her time, Gaye quilts less. Yet she continues to study the history of quiltmaking, building a library of reference books on the subjects of quilts and Southern material culture.

Gaye Rice Ingram, Louisiana. *Submitted.*

When her children graduated from college, she began to add to her collection of quilts. A teacher both by profession and inclination, Gaye has worked to encourage the study of early quilts and quiltmaking among people in her region, where, she says, "Folks would rather make quilts than study quilts." With fellow American Quilt Study member Carolyn Roller Miller, of Texas, she organized a regional quilt study group to study quilts of the South, and with the help of members Kathy Moore and Laurel Horton, she initiated the Southern Quilt Conference, which has drawn attendance from across the country. She has curated exhibitions, published articles, and edited *Blanket Statements*, the AQSG newsletter. A lifelong student and teacher of the literature and culture of the American South, she is particularly interested in Southern quilts.

Gaye attributes her early interest in sewing and the needle arts to her mother, a skilled seamstress and needlewoman. More recently, she points to the American Quilt Study Group and the Quilt History List, an Internet group monitored by Kris Driessen, as critical agents in her own study, saying they "created communities that have helped me explore the history of quiltmaking, that nurtured a passion I otherwise might have been denied." Noting Sue Wildemuth's signal importance to her quiltmaking, she says, "Sue's unexpected invitation to participate in her Eagle Project returned me to quiltmaking, showing me how much might be achieved in small quilts and how much might be learned in making them. It opened a new world for me, made my fingers itch for more." For encouraging her to accept this invitation and for sharing fabric and laughter at critical stages of its progress, she credits quilters Lorie Stubbs and Lynn Lancaster Gorges, whose work she admires.

*1850s Eagle*, 1850 to 1859, 9" x 9", Kate Adams, Maine. Collection of Author. *Photograph by Best Days Photography.*

# 1850s Eagle

Using antique fabrics and early patterns and designs, Kate Adams creates miniature quilts that are truly reflective of the art of traditional American quiltmaking. Her designs are inspired by nineteenth and twentieth century quilts and are carefully adapted to a scale of one inch equals one foot (1:12). Many hours are involved in the drafting, fabric selection, cutting, and making of the initial piece. This accomplished, quilts are then recreated using antique fabrics.

**Quilt Technique:** Hand sewing work and embroidery.

For this particular project, Kate researched and chose the 1850s eagle motif. She discovered that some patriotic quilts created from 1850 to 1859 contained the design motifs of the flag, an eagle, arrows, laurel leaves, and a shield, so she incorporated these motifs into her piece and called this amazing work of art *1850s Eagles*.

Detail, *1850s Eagle,* Maine. Four-block upper right corner eagle close-up. Collection of Author. *Photograph by Best Days Photography.*

# Kate Adams

Kate Adams, Maine. *Submitted.*

Kate Adams' interest in quiltmaking was fostered at a very early age by her mother and grandmother. Accomplished needleworkers, they passed on their love of textiles to Kate. In the rural Northern California dairy farming community in which she was born and reared, Kate says needlework skills were held in high regard. These skills, learned at home and in the local 4-H Club, helped her acquire an apprenticeship with a local costume maker. Along with her years as a volunteer in small community theaters, this experience helped her develop her skills and a personal style.

A chance request for a one inch scale quilt for a young friend's doll house launched Kate onto the path that she is following today. Once again employing her love of nineteenth century style quilts and her interest in history, she developed designs to market to adult collectors of finely crafted one inch scale miniatures. In 1989, Kate was asked to display her work at a traditional American folk art show in Pennsylvania. "For this event, I opted to use remnants from my collection of antique fabrics and to present my work matted and framed," she says. "I thought this might appeal to a broader audience and add an air of authenticity and uniqueness to the pieces." This new approach proved to be a springboard for Kate's future success. Today, the miniature quilts of Kate Adams are in many of the finest private collections of folk art in America, Japan, and Europe.

**Website:** *Kate Adams Fine Miniature Quilts.*
www.kateadamsfineminiaturequilts.com

*Eagle Medallion*, 1860 to 1869, 22" x 22.25", Lisa Ruetz, Michigan. Collection of Author. *Photograph by Best Days Photography.*

# Eagle Medallion

When Susan asked me to be a part of this project, I chose the 1860s as the decade I would represent in my quilt. The period of 1830 to 1860 is my favorite period for quilts, fabrics, and clothing. I especially love children's clothing from this time period.

Looking for inspiration, I browsed through my quilt history books. I found that inspiration on page 123 of *The American Quilt: A History of Cloth and Comfort 1750 to 1950* by Roderick Kiracofe. I was looking for something that would not only represent the period, but would also be somewhat challenging to make. This four block eagle quilt was the perfect inspiration for my *Eagle Medallion* quilt. You can't go wrong with red and green, and I loved the busyness of the design. My quilt is appliquéd with cottons, and in keeping with the period, the embroidery is with silk thread.

*– Lisa Ruetz*

**Quilt Technique:** Appliqué, hand piecing and hand quilting, and embroidery.

Detail, *Eagle Medallion,* Michigan. Eagle close-up. Collection of Author. *Photograph by Best Days Photography.*

Detail, *Eagle Medallion,* Michigan. Applique and quilting close-up. Collection of Author. *Photograph by Best Days Photography.*

# Lisa Ruetz

Lisa Ruetz, Michigan. *Submitted*

Lisa Ruetz is a quilt and doll maker who also is interested in the history of quilts, dolls, and textiles. Drawn to needlework since childhood, she has worked in many of its forms. She enjoys using antique or reproduction textiles to recreate antique quilts, working only by hand because she finds serenity in the rhythm of needle and thread. Although she pieces occasionally, her heart inclines toward appliqué, and she has a particular interest in Baltimore Album Quilts.

Lisa has made antique reproduction dolls for several years, mainly in cloth or wood, and particularly enjoys creating period clothing for them. She enjoys attending classes and retreats across the country to learn new painting and doll making techniques.

Lisa belongs to the Midwest Fabric Study Group, the West Michigan Quilt History Study Group, and the American Quilt Study Group. She enjoys researching antique quilts and textiles for her blogs, *Stray Threads* and *Material Witness*. She is also a team member of *Glorious Appliqué*.

Lisa lives in Michigan, and shares her love of quilts with her three cats, Rufus, Brody, and Teague. Her non-sewing interests include genealogy, antiquing, and cooking. She is teaching herself stumpwork.

**Blogs:** *Stray Threads.* quilltr.blogspot.com/ *Material Witness.* material-witness.blogspot.com/ *Glorious Appliqué.* gloriousapplique.blogspot.com/

# The Civil War, Eagles, and Quilts

## Bets Ramsey

*Four Block Eagle Quilt*, South Carolina, c. 1850. Cotton (66.5" x 68.5"). Parks Wildemuth Collection. *Photograph by Best Days Photography.*

Bets Ramsey, Tennessee

When Rebecah Foster completed her Eagle Quilt on October 5, 1808, in Nashville, Tennessee, she had appliquéd seventeen fabric links of chain and within them named the seventeen states of the Union. The nation was thirty-two years old and Tennessee had been a part of it for thirteen years. More than likely, Rebecah made the quilt for her wedding, and we can assume that it was saved for special occasions because it is still in good condition after two hundred years. Who knew in 1861 that an American citizen, a Southern woman, had proclaimed patriotic allegiance to her country by making a bold eagle-emblazoned quilt long before the country was to be torn apart?

Tennessee was one of the states that did not immediately secede from the Union at the beginning of the Civil War because of divided loyalties. Later, when the state did vote to secede, Nashville became the first state capitol to be occupied by the northern army and remain under siege for the duration of the war. Was Rebecah, probably in her seventies then, still alive? What did she do with her quilt while both armies continually fought, gained, lost, and regained ground all across the state? So fierce was the turmoil that only Virginia saw more battles than Tennessee. Someone did safely secure the eagle quilt, symbol of the hated enemy, from being confiscated as a war souvenir.

In the 1850s, unrest was stirring across the nation over the slavery issue, with its many moral, political, and economic ramifications. The outbreak of "The War Between the States" brought action by the individual states to announce their stand with or against the Union. Those states nearest the Mason Dixon Line were more divided in their loyalty than the states in the deep South.

Detail, *Four Block Eagle Quilt*, hand-appliqué block depicting eagles and border. Parks Wildemuth Collection. *Photograph Courtesy of Randy Lee Marshall.*

It was not unknown for families to have sons fighting on opposite sides. The Southern states were able to unify their efforts by forming the Confederate States of America and waging war on the Union forces.

Neither the North nor the South was prepared for an extensive military encounter that supplied the equipment necessary for a widely scattered operation. Where military supplies were unavailable, soldiers' families made uniforms, flags, company banners, and bedding. Women's diaries describe the sewing, knitting, weaving, and making-do that was required to overcome the shortage of supplies as the war raged on.

Nevertheless, in all the strife and turmoil of war, human kindness did arise, even at the risk of death. One woman and her teenaged daughter living in a rural Southern county, with husband and sons gone to war, dared to chance a sentence of treason by taking in a young wounded Yankee soldier, hiding him in the attic, and nursing him back to health. Eventually he found his way back to his home in New York State. A few years later, his family sent a red, white, and blue Rocky Mountain Road quilt they made as a thank you gift to the brave women who had tended his wounds.

After the defeat of the Confederate Army, it was years before many southerners would display an eagle or an American flag, so deep were the scars of the Civil War.

—*Bets Ramsey, Tennessee*

## 1870 to 1879

*Remembering Grant*, 1870 to 1879, 25" x 25", Susan Wildemuth, Illinois. Collection of Author. *Photograph by Best Days Photography.*

# Remembering Grant

With my eagle motif piece, I chose to honor President U.S. Grant, the 1870s, and Illinois. The inspiration for this project came from a trip I took in the summer of 2010 to Galena, Illinois, for a family reunion. My brothers and their families drove in from various parts of Iowa and Illinois to spend a weekend in five cabins on the edge of town and to visit some historic places. There are still spots in Galena that haven't changed since the time Grant walked the streets there. Grant's home still exists as a historic site on a hill overlooking this historic community.

I created this piece from the center out, using fat quarters, antique textiles, buttons (antique and new), and computer photo transfer sheets. I used an eagle printed on reproduction fabric from Sara Morgan's Old Glory Line for Blue Hill Fabrics. This repeating eagle fabric came in several color choices, and I chose tan. I framed one cutout eagle with coordinating blue and tan star fabric. This is my second attempt at an art quilt, though I've been creating traditional quilts since the 1980s.

**Quilt Technique:** Hand pieced and hand quilted, appliqué, and piecing.

# Susan Wildemuth

Susan Wildemuth, Illinois. *Submitted.*

I was born Susan Eileen Parks in a small Iowa community, but I have lived most of my adult life in Illinois on our grain farm near Geneseo, Illinois. Creating is an essential part of my life. Whether it is quilting, refinishing furniture, cooking, or writing, I am defined by two things, creative work and my family.

My mother would tell you I was born into the world wanting to know "why." I imagine my endless questions are the reason she has white hair. In a college course in General Education, I learned I had a personality type of INFJ, based on the BFN personality test. This means that loyalty is important to me, that no one could sell me swampland unless I wanted to own it, and that I notice things. For example, did *you* notice, my initials are S.E.W.?

Quilting came into my life back in 1985, when I signed up for a quilting class with the hope that quilting, unlike the oil painting classes I had been taking for three years, would fulfill a creative ache in me.

On the second night of class, the quilt teacher said, "I will be able to tell you, halfway through this class, who will continue to quilt once this class is done," and then she turned to me and said, "I don't have to wait until then to tell you, you love this, don't you?" She was right. I had found what I was looking for.

Detail, *Remembering Grant,* Illinois. Center medallion President U.S. Grant and Mrs. Julia Dent Grant with antique G.A.R. button. Collection of Author. *Photograph by Best Days Photography.*

My interest in quilt history surfaced when I attended the Illinois Quilt Research Project at the old Colony School in Bishop Hill, Illinois. There, I met a senior quilter and quilt collector with two laundry baskets overflowing with antique quilts. I was impressed that this dear soul knew the provenance of each one of her quilts. There is truth in the adage "When student is ready, the teacher will come." Not only did this woman impress upon me the importance of documenting quilts, but she also was the first person to introduce me to the concept of dating quilts through the use of pattern design, colors, and fabrics. Meeting this woman, whose name I never learned, changed my life. I became interested in researching, writing, and sharing quilt and quilt history stories.

In the 1990s, I discovered The American Quilt Study Group and later Kris Driessen's Quilt History Internet List, where I found like-minded people who loved quilts and quilt history as much as I did. Along with Marilyn Woodin and Catherine Litwinow, in 2003 I founded the Iowa Illinois Quilt Study Group, which makes its home base at the Kalona Quilt and Textile Museum in Kalona, Iowa. I served in various positions in that group until 2007.

My purpose in starting my *Illinois Quilt History* website was to document, save, and share Illinois Quilt History stories. I like the Internet website venue because it allows people to update information so that information is current. I started a companion blog a year later because I like the conversational, flow-of-thought format. It is like sitting across the table from one of your neighbors and having a chat over a cup of coffee. Interesting things get said. My book shelves are filled with quilt history books. Those tactile treasures are not just "for pretty." I read them cover-to-cover. I believe learning is a lifetime job.

In my non-quilting writing life, my work has been featured in a variety of publications from magazines in the areas of history, agriculture, humor, and current events to newspapers with my life lessons column, where I start with a quotation and then share a story that relates to it. In my quilt writing life I have written for *Quilt, Quilt World, Country Quilting, Quick and Easy Quilting, Antique Quilts, Quilter's World, Pieces of Time,* and *PieceWork* magazines.

The short version of my quilting biography might be summarized thus:

*Susan Wildemuth is an author, researcher, and quilting aficionado. Her research, writing, and photographs have been published in national, regional, and local quilt and textile history publications. The areas of her quilt history research are Eagle Quilts, Bicentennial Quilts, LeeWards, Collingbourne Mills, Boag Ribboncraft, and Illinois quilt history.*

**Website:** *Illinois Quilt History: Quilt History from the Midwest.* www.illinoisquilthistory.com/
**Blog:** *Eye of the Needle: Quilt History Conversation from the Midwest.*
sew-eyeoftheneedlequilthistory.blogspot.com

*1880s Eagle*, 1880 to 1889, 21" x 21", Don Beld, California. Machine Embroidery by Bernice Foster. Collection of Author. *Photograph by Best Days Photography.*

# 1880s Eagle

A quilt artist and historian, Don Beld is the founder and guiding force behind the Home of the Brave Quilt Project, which delivers replicas of quilts made for Civil War soldiers to the families of the Fallen Heroes from Iraq and Afghanistan. This is an on-going project.

In 2010, Don was featured in one of the chapters in a book written by Joe Cunningham, entitled *Men and the Art of Quiltmaking*. Mr. Beld and Pam Weeks have coauthored a book of their own, entitled *Civil War Quilts*.

Sharing his inspiration for this quilt Don says:

*Indigo blue and white quilts were a fad in the 1880s as were eagle quilts because the decade marked the 100th Anniversary of the signing of the Constitution and the formation of the United States of America. Small eight-pointed star blocks were also popular in this time. The hand quilting is done on a one-half inch and one-third inch grid. Bernice Foster machined embroidered the eagle and the wording in the center medallion. The binding was done in a traditional nineteenth century straight edge, with rounded corners binding.*

**Quilt Technique:** Hand piecing and hand quilting by Don Beld with machine embroidery by Bernice Foster.

Detail, *1880s Eagle*, California. Eagle close-up, machine embroidery by Bernice Foster. Collection of Author. *Photograph by Best Days Photography.*

# Don Beld

Don Beld, California. *Submitted.*

Founder of the Home of the Brave Quilt Project, in 2004, Don Beld has used needlework since the days of Rosey Grier, in the late 1970s, as a stress management technique from his regular job as a behavioral health hospital administrator. In 1992, he transitioned to quilting after taking a traditional twelve-week hand-piecing and hand-quilting class in Campbell, California.

Because of his interest in American history, Don works almost exclusively with nineteenth century reproduction fabrics and pieced quilt patterns. Recognized as one of the nation's experts on U.S. Sanitary Commission (USSC) quilts, Don has carried his passion forward by making versions of existing USSC quilts.

Don was a featured artist at the 2007 Road to California Quilt Show, in Ontario, California. Some of Don's works are featured in the ground-breaking work, *Men and the Art of Quiltmaking*, an AQS publication, 2010, and he presented a program on his September 11, 2001, quilts, entitled "Remembering With Honor: Quilters Salute Their Heroes," at the 2011 annual American Quilt Study Group Seminar. A special exhibit features these quilts as well as Don's September 11, 2001, quilts in the Educational Gallery at the International Quilt Study Center Museum in Lincoln, Nebraska, from October 2012 to January 2013. *Excerpt from* Civil War Quilts *Don Beld and Pam Weeks (Schiffer Publishing).*

*Pennsylvania Eagle 1890*, 1890 to 1899, 23.25" x 23.25", Barbara Garrett, Pennsylvania. Collection of Author. *Photograph by Best Days Photography.*

# Pennsylvania Eagle 1890

I live in southeastern Pennsylvania and taught myself to quilt by studying antique Pennsylvania German quilts from my region. One of my favorites is a style I call "the four block eagle quilt." Quilts in this style contain four large eagles, set diagonally with wings stretched out wide, almost touching, in the four corners of the quilt. Each has a shield on its breast. They have distinctive legs and usually have something in their beaks that some have theorized is a firecracker or cigar.

I chose this style eagle for my project because it represents my favorite time period of quilt making, the last two decades of the nineteenth century. I love the color palate used by Pennsylvania German quiltmakers during this time period. The bright crayon colors of red, green, and cheddar are typical colors for this eagle pattern, which is why I chose them for my quilt. The backgrounds of local appliquéd quilts from the late 1800s are usually a light colored print or shirting. I chose a double blue background because the color was very popular in quilts during this time and is often identified with quilts from this area of Pennsylvania.

*– Barbara Garrett*

**Quilt Technique:** Appliqué and hand piecing and quilting.

Detail, *Pennsylvania Eagle 1890*, Pennsylvania. Eagle view. Collection of Author. *Photograph by Best Days Photography.*

Pennsylvania

9

# Barbara Garrett

Barbara Garrett, Pennsylvania. *Submitted.*

A self-taught quilter, Barbara Garrett has studied antique quilts from southeastern Pennsylvania for inspiration and knowledge of quilting techniques since 1969. Preferring traditional patterns, Barbara uses both antique and reproduction fabrics to recreate the styles and appearance of the period from 1800 to 1950 in both full-sized and doll quilts.

Becoming involved in quilt documentation in the 1980s, she worked on documentation projects in Berks, Bucks, Chester, Montgomery, Delaware, and Franklin counties in Pennsylvania and served as a consultant for projects in Schuylkill and York counties. She is a volunteer with the Delaware State Quilt Documentation Project and was a consultant for the Kent County, Maryland, project. She is also one of the authors of the York County Documentation book, *Quilts: The Fabric of Friendship*, published in 2001.

Barbara's doll quilts have appeared in *A Quiltie Ladies Garden Journal*, published by the Variable Star Quilters; *A Quilt Block Challenge: Vintage Revisited*, published by Schiffer Books; and *Miniature Quilts* magazine. A queen-sized quilt she designed and made from feedsack fabric was the demonstration quilt on an episode of HGTV's *Simply Quilts*, hosted by Alex Anderson. As the featured guest on another *Simply Quilts* episode, Barbara discussed Pennsylvania German quilts of the late 1800s and demonstrated how to make her Joseph's Coat doll quilt pattern.

A member of the American Quilt Study Group, Barbara has presented a Study Center at an AQSG Seminar. She is a volunteer docent and demonstrator at the Lancaster Quilt and Textile Museum. In 2008 and 2010, she curated shows of privately owned antique quilts for the Historic Poole Forge in Churchtown, Pennsylvania. In 2011, she worked with the Germantown Historical Society in Philadelphia to cohost a Quilt Turning of the quilts in the Society collection.

Barbara began creating her collection of reproduction doll quilts in 1980. Using patterns, she has published for doll quilts in her collection; she now teaches classes at seminars and quilt guilds on making doll quilts. She continues to speak on various aspects of quilt history to quilt guilds and historical societies, sharing her collections of reproduction doll quilts and antique quilts.

*Eagle in a New Century*, 1900 to 1909, 24" x 24", Deborah S. Rake, Texas. Collection of Author.
*Photograph by Best Days Photography.*

# Eagle in a New Century

Debby chose the 1900s as her decade because it posed a challenge. "A number of eras immediately bring to mind a distinctive style, such as 1880s crazy quilts, 1930s Depression styles, and the double knits of the 1960s, but I could not easily call to mind an image of a quilt made at the turn of the last century," she says. "I looked at a great many quilts in the International Quilt Study Center (IQSC) database and recalled learning in one of my classes that wool crazies, embellished with cotton embroidery in simple feather stitches, continued to be made long after the fashion for the elegant and time-consuming silk crazies had faded. My choice was made." Debby chose to employ embroidery techniques to create her eagles and add details to the fabric pieces in her interpretation of a 1900s crazy quilt.

This beautiful piece tells the story of a slice of time in American history when average women lived a work-laden existence. Nonetheless, these resourceful souls still found a way to feed their creative natures and keep their families warm.

**Quilt Technique:** Hand embroidery and machine piecing.

Detail, *Eagle in a New Century,* Texas. Eagle view. Collection of Author. *Photograph by Best Days Photography.*

# Deborah S. Rake

Deborah S. Rake, Texas. *Submitted.*

Deborah S. Rake decided she needed a new bedspread, and the local fabric store in her small town community offered a class in quilting. That confluence started Deborah on the road to quiltmaking. Her first piece was made in the Rail Fence pattern. More classes and workshops followed, and at one of these—a three-day workshop in Omaha, Nebraska—the course of her life was changed.

That workshop featured quilt and textile history speakers. Debby explains, "I was able to meet experienced, expert quilters and to see the elaborate quilts they created. Around that same time I heard that the University of Nebraska at Lincoln was offering a Masters Degree in Quilt History. In August of that same year, I enrolled in the program."

She spent the next five years working toward her degree, and it was a wonderful time in her life. Debby says, "I not only learned about quilts themselves, but also about their importance as artifacts in the study of women's history. Art or studio quilting was another revelation."

*In God We Trust, Two*, 1910 to 1919, 23" x 23", Connie Chunn, Missouri. Collection of Author. *Photograph by Best Days Photography.*

# In God We Trust, Two

The inspiration for this piece can be found in *The Quilt Index* and was a part of the Hawaiian Quilt Research Project. The name of the original, c. 1918, is *In God We Trust*.

The quilt was constructed using:

**1.** 100 percent cotton fabrics.
**2.** 100 percent cotton Warm and White batting.
**3.** YLI Quilting Thread, color Natural No. 1, 100-percent Glazed Cotton, my favorite brand because it does not tangle easily.
**4.** A quilting pattern similar to that in the 1918 full-sized artifact; a cotton muslin back.

**Quilt Technique:** Hand piecing and quilting, embroidery, and fabric printing on center square.

Detail, *In God We Trust, Two, center medallion, Missouri. Eagle view.* Missouri. Collection of Author. *Photograph by Best Days Photography.*

Connie Chunn, Missouri. *Submitted.*

## Connie Chunn

Designer Connie Chunn has been an active quilter since 1975. She specializes in making miniatures. Several of her miniature quilts have won ribbons in national shows like the International Quilters Association show in Houston, the Vermont Quilt Festival, Quilt America!, the National Quilters Association show, and the Miniatures From the Heart contest. Connie's miniatures have also been juried into the American Quilter's Society quilt show at Paducah, Kentucky, as well as having been published in *Miniature Quilts* magazine. Issue 62 of *Miniature Quilts* magazine contains a four-page interview with Connie about the creation of these small quilts.

As a historian, Connie is an authority on the history and patterns of the Ladies Art Company (1889 to 1974) of St. Louis, Missouri.

**Website:** *Ladies Art Company.* www.ladiesartcompany.com

*Red Cross: A Symbol of Hope*, 1910 to 1919, 26.25" x 25.5", Kimberly Wulfert, Ph.D., California, and Susan Wildemuth, Illinois. Collection of Author. *Photograph by Best Days Photography.*

# Red Cross: A Symbol of Hope

Hope plus Help plus Service equals The American Red Cross.

Phase one of this piece began its life in Kimberly Wulfert's studio in California. Kim chose the colors in 100 percent cotton fabrics, and designed the layout of the quilt. The Red Cross and alternating blocks with eagle images were machine pieced and assembled. She added a double border and then sent it on to me in Illinois for completion.

Phase two of the creative process began with the addition of some American Red Cross artifacts from Kim's collection and some from mine. Some were historic pieces, such as a yellow veil worn by a Red Cross worker. Using a computer printer and treated fabric sheets, I also reproduced a 1910s postcard from Kim's collection.

The artifacts were selected, arranged, and appliquéd to the quilt top in order to tell a story and to provide insights into the organization's work. Dream Cotton was our batting choice, and the piece was finished with crosshatch hand quilting.

Our goal was to honor and dedicate this quilt to an organization we both admire. We called our joint effort *Red Cross: A Symbol of Hope*.

*— Susan Wildemuth*

**Quilt Technique:** Machine piecing, hand appliqué, hand quilting, and photo fabric image reproduction.

Detail, *Red Cross: A Symbol of Hope*, California and Illinois. Center quilt close-up. Collection of Author. *Photograph by Best Days Photography.*

Kimberly Wulfert, Ph.D., California. *Submitted. Photography by Caitlin Jean Petersen.*

## Kimberly Wulfert, Ph.D.

Psychologist Kimberly Wulfert, Ph.D., is an author, researcher, artist, and quilt expert. Her research and writing have been published in national, regional, and local quilt and textile history publications. Her areas of expertise are nineteenth century quilts, John Hewson, and dating antique and vintage quilts.

**Websites:** *New Pathways Into Quilt History.* www.antiquequiltdating.com/; *Antique Quilt Dating Guides by Style.* www.antiquequiltdatingguides.com/
**Blog:** *Quilters Spirit.* quiltersspirit.blogspot.com

Susan Wildemuth, Illinois. *Submitted.*

## Susan Wildemuth

Susan Wildemuth is an author, researcher, and quilting aficionado. Her research, writing, and photography have been published in national, regional, and local quilt and textile history publications. Her areas of quilt history research are Eagle Quilts, Bicentennial Quilts, LeeWards, Collingbourne Mills, Boag Ribboncraft, and Illinois quilt history.

**Websites:** *Illinois Quilt History: Quilt History from the Midwest.* www.illinoisquilthistory.com/
**Blog:** *Eye of the Needle: Quilt History Conversation from the Midwest.* sew-eyeoftheneedlequilthistory.blogspot.com/

*Little Lone Eagle*, 1920 to 1929, 16.5" x 20.5", Susan Price Miller, Kentucky. Collection of Author. *Photograph by Best Days Photography.*

# Little Lone Eagle

I enjoyed making this miniature reproduction of Emma Tyrrell's *Lone Eagle* quilt. The pattern is significant because we know exactly how she created it, a rare thing for a quilt pattern, especially in the first part of the twentieth century. The pattern commemorated a significant event, Lindbergh's 1927 non-stop solo flight across the Atlantic, which captured the world's imagination. Charles Lindbergh's nickname, "the Lone Eagle," inspired both the name of the quilt and the bold and detailed eagle motif Tyrrell prescribed for the quilting pattern and for the embroidered eagles found in the setting squares.

Emma Tyrrell's accurate airplane block and eagle design have been popular since they first appeared in the January 1929 issue of *Successful Farming*. Pilot and quilt collector Rägi Marino found more than twenty publications that included a quilt design either based on this pattern or made directly from the original pattern. In one publication, *Quilt World*, February 1983, Ruby Duncan copied the *Successful Farming* article and provided full-sized patterns.

While flying in a 747 plane to and from Chile in November 2010, I used Duncan's eagle motif, reduced to fit a four-inch block, and embroidered several eagles. The new miniature appeared in the Tulip Time Quilt Show of the Pella Area Quilters Guild on May 4, 2011, exactly one year and one day from the date the project proposal arrived in my e-mail.

– *Susan Price Miller*

**Quilt Technique:** Hand quilting and piecing and embroidery.

Detail, *Little Lone Eagle*, Kentucky. Alternating pieced airplane and embroidered eagle blocks. Collection of Author. *Photograph by Best Days Photography.*

Susan Price Miller, Kentucky. *Submitted.*

## Susan Price Miller

Susan Price Miller says:

*I was born in 1940, spent my first decade in West Virginia, the second in Connecticut, the third in Indiana and Illinois, and the next four decades in Pella, Iowa. I majored in history and minored in math at DePauw University in Greencastle, Indiana. At Milliken University in Decatur, Illinois, I studied studio art for three years. These interests, plus a long background in sewing, all came together in the realm of quilts. Around 1980, I joined a group of hand quilters at the Second Reformed Church in Pella, Iowa. In addition to teaching me how to quilt on a floor frame, the members told me intriguing stories about their lives in Pella.*

While learning about the history of local quiltmaking, Susan came across the name Carlie Sexton. Cuesta Benberry's assurance that Ms. Sexton was important to the development of American quiltmaking and Benberry's subsequent research encouragement led to Susan's first paper, published in *Uncoverings* by the American Quilt Study Group in 1996. Three more related papers for AQSG came out of that original research.

*Meanwhile, Susan says: I was also designing quilt patterns, teaching classes, participating in the Pella Area Quilters Guild, and writing articles for* American Patchwork & Quilting *magazine and Meredith's "bookazine"* Century of Quilts, *published in 2002. At present, I spend a lot of time studying a small collection of quilts and a large collection of paintings at the Scholte House Museum, the home of the founder of Pella. In 2010, I produced a small book about a woman's memories of her childhood in the late 1800s. I hope to write more stories related to Pella history and to make more reproductions of antique American and Dutch quilts.*

*NRA Blue Eagle Sampler*, 1930 to 1939, 22.5" x 22.5", Leigh Fellner, Massachusetts. Collection of Author. *Photograph by Best Days Photography.*

# NRA Blue Eagle Sampler

This quilt was created by quilt artist, designer, researcher, writer, and historian Leigh Fellner of Hart Cottage Quilts. The first quilt artist and historian contacted about this project, Leigh agreed to produce a quilt including a NRA Blue Eagle.

Leigh's design features a reverse appliquéd NRA Blue Eagle as the center medallion. The center medallion is surrounded by quilt blocks from patterns that might have been used by 1930s quiltmakers. Leigh used actual c. 1930 to 1935 fabrics in constructing the quilt top and feedsack fabric for the backing of this piece. The batting is Hobbs Heirloom cotton poly blend, and the piece is machine quilted with polyester thread.

The National Recovery Administration (NRA) was a key New Deal agency established in 1933, early in the first administration of President Franklin D. Roosevelt. Its purpose was to eliminate what Roosevelt called "destructive competition" in business by bringing members of industry, labor, and government together to establish "codes of fair competition." These codes set minimum wages and maximum weekly hours for workers and established minimum prices for products. The NRA was highly publicized, and goods produced by participating industries were stamped with the ubiquitous blue eagle and the motto "We Do Our Part." The NRA was short-lived, lasting only through 1935, when it was declared unconstitutional on the grounds that it violated the separation of the powers under the Constitution. By then, however, its blue icon was perhaps better known throughout the country than symbols of other, longer lasting New Deal programs.

**Quilt Technique:** Hand appliqué and piecing, machine piecing and reverse appliqué, and machine quilting.

Detail, *NRA Blue Eagle Sampler,* Massachusetts. NRA Eagle, reverse appliqué. Collection of Author. *Photograph by Susan Wildemuth.*

## Leigh Fellner

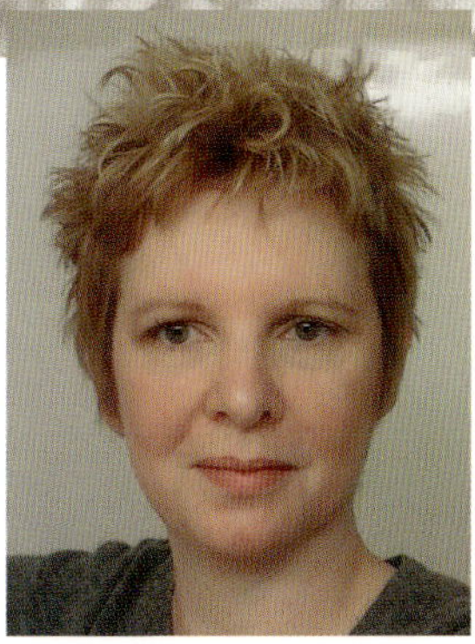

Leigh Fellner, Massachusetts. *Submitted.*

Quilt historian Leigh Fellner is probably best known for debunking the myth of the Underground Railroad "quilt codes" propagated by some quilt historians and for her series of articles on African textiles of the slave trade era and their relation to African-American quilts.

The quilt designer Leigh Fellner is best known for her miniature quilts made from authentic 1825 to 1875 antique and vintage cottons. Her pieces have been featured in *Quilt, Country Quilts, Small Quilts, Sampler Quilts* and *Log & Timber Style* magazines. Several of Leigh's pieces are in the art collection of the Neutrogena Corporation in Los Angeles.

**Website:** *Hart Cottage Quilts.* hartcottagequilts.com

# Eleanor Roosevelt 1935

## "Thank You for the Quilt" Letter

My dad admired Eleanor Roosevelt and I have to admit, I'm a fan of hers, too. A person of action, she was a good citizen of the world, respected and admired for her intelligence and work ethic throughout her entire life.

Those of us who study twentieth century quilt history know Eleanor Roosevelt was the lucky recipient of many quilts during FDR's White House years. Did you ever wonder if she actually received and then acknowledged those wonderful gifts?

She did.

Besides antique, vintage, and new eagle quilts, I collect antique and vintage quilt ephemera (paper) of all kinds. In January 2011, this February 9, 1935, letter, written on official White House stationery and signed by Eleanor Roosevelt while her husband, Franklin D. Roosevelt was president, found a new home with me. It's a thank you note to a Mrs. Jules Joseph Fischer (of Mountain View, California), Mrs. McGrath, and "the rest of the ladies" for a quilt they made and sent to her.

Let's see what Mrs. Roosevelt had to say:

*THE WHITE HOUSE,*
*WASHINGTON*
*February 9, 1935,*

*My dear Mrs. Fischer:*

*I was very much delighted to receive from Mrs. McGrath the quilt which you and all the other women so generously made for me. It is very lovely, and I greatly appreciate the work and thought which you have all put into it.*

*With many thanks and all good wishes, I am*

*Very sincerely yours,*
*Eleanor Roosevelt*

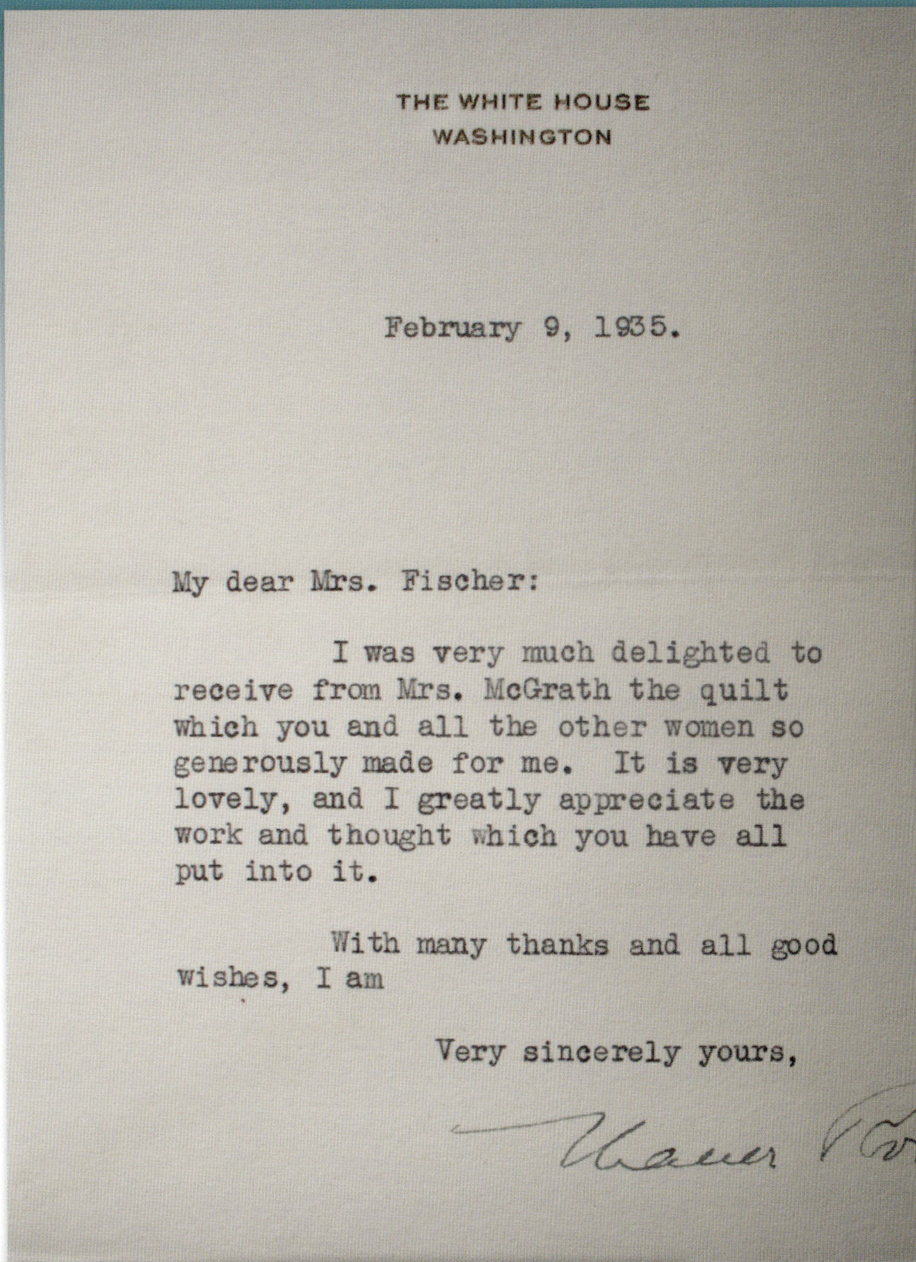

THE WHITE HOUSE
WASHINGTON

February 9, 1935.

My dear Mrs. Fischer:

I was very much delighted to receive from Mrs. McGrath the quilt which you and all the other women so generously made for me. It is very lovely, and I greatly appreciate the work and thought which you have all put into it.

With many thanks and all good wishes, I am

Very sincerely yours,

Eleanor Roosevelt. Collection of Author.

Letter From First Lady Eleanor Roosevelt to Mrs. Jules Joseph Fischer of Mountain View, California, February 9, 1935. Collection of Author. *Photograph by Susan Wildemuth.*

THE WHITE HOUSE
WASHINGTON

WASHINGTON D.C.
FEB 12
2-PM
1935

Mrs. Jules Joseph Fischer
Mountain View
California

Envelope of the Letter from First Lady Eleanor Roosevelt to Mrs. Jules Joseph Fischer of Mountain View, California, Postmarked February 12, 1935. Collection of Author. *Photograph by Susan Wildemuth.*

*The Eagle: Walter Carlin Parks, Jr.*, 1940 to 1949, 40" x 60", Susan Wildemuth, Illinois. Collection of Author. *Photograph by Best Days Photography.*

# The Eagle: Walter Carlin Parks, Jr.

I made this quilt for my dad, Walter Carlin Parks, Jr., who is "the eagle."

I have been a traditional quilter, hand piecer, and quilter since 1985. Although I never thought I would venture into the arena of art quilts, I have always been drawn to pictorial quilts that tell stories. When, in 2010, I decided to try my hand at creating an art quilt, I knew the piece would have to tell a story, incorporate my love of history, and include an eagle motif.

A defining moment is a point at which the essential nature or character of a person is revealed or identified and as a result of this moment, event, or discovery, the person's life is changed forever. Like that of so many others in his generation, my dad's defining moment was World War II. The lady pictured to his right, the good-looking one, is my mom, Betty Parks.

Do you see the aircraft carrier on fire worked into the Storm at Sea quilt pattern? Reproduced with the help of my computer and a fabric photo sheet, that is an actual photograph of my dad's ship, the *St. Lo*, at the moment it was hit by enemy fire in the Battle of Leyte Gulf off the Philippine Islands.

As a not-so-final word about art quilts, I love the no-rules aspect of art quilts. The maker can use anything in them from buttons to string to fabric to thread to ribbons to photographs. The lack of conventional rules frees her up to create and tell a story she desires. Sharing and saving, I'm all about the story.

**Quilt Technique:** Hand piecing and appliqué, photo fabric reproduction, embroidery, and hand quilting.

Detail, *The Eagle: Walter Carlin Parks, Jr.*, depiction of the aircraft carrier *St. Lo* at the moment of impact from enemy fire using fabric photo reproduction with hand-pieced airplanes worked into four Storm at Sea quilt blocks. *Photograph by Susan Wildemuth.*

## Susan Wildemuth

Susan Wildemuth, Illinois. *Submitted.*

Susan Wildemuth is an author, researcher, and quilting aficionado. Her research, writing, and photographs have been published in national, regional, and local quilt and textile history publications. Her areas of quilt history research are Eagle Quilts, Bicentennial Quilts, LeeWards, Collingbourne Mills, Boag Ribboncraft, and Illinois quilt history.

**Website:** *Illinois Quilt History: Quilt History from the Midwest.*
www.illinoisquilthistory.com/
**Blog:** *Eye of the Needle: Quilt History Conversation from the Midwest.*
sew-eyeoftheneedlequilthistory.blogspot.com

# Pearl Harbor December 7, 1941

## Gaye Rice Ingram

Detail, United States Navy motif badge, c. 1940. Parks Wildemuth Collection. *Photograph by Susan Wildemuth.*

It was a cloudless, blue Sunday, and the island was just rousing from untroubled sleep. Along the lanes leading down to the harbor, palm-shaded homes had opened their doors and windows to the tropical ocean breezes. Neither automobile nor bicycle nor human being yet moved on those roads. Below, in the great harbor, the early sun glanced off the big battleships and destroyers at anchor there, their flags not yet raised. Dockside, all was still. When the first sounds of airplane engines were heard, Army medics making routine sickbay rounds laughed: those crazy marines were at it again, maneuvering even on a Sunday! Then the tropical world turned black with the smoke from burning ships, and the pristine waters of Pearl Harbor became a fiery lake of burning oil. The wail of air raid sirens, the unending roar of wave after wave of low-flying aircraft, and the explosions of bunker bursting bombs filled the world. In the hills above the harbor, wives of American naval officers stationed at Pearl Harbor looked up into the faces of the Japanese pilots flying those planes, saw them smile as they banked, and turned again toward the inferno below.

Gaye Rice Ingram, Louisiana

Within hours, the United States mainland was bracing for the attack everyone knew would follow. San Francisco seemed the most likely first target, and that night the city went dark. Motorists were ordered off the streets, and those who had to drive used only their parking lights. Across the country, fear seized the nation. No one was safe. The next attack could come anywhere, at any time, at New Orleans or Mobile, Boston, or New York. Rumors ran rampant: Japanese troops had come ashore in Southern California; New Jersey harbors had been mined; Japanese battleships and aircraft carriers now blockaded the Panama Canal.

The fear that transfixed the nation on December 7, 1941, was different from anything any living American had known. Vast oceans separated America from the rest of the world, protecting it since 1812 from foreign invasion. Now, suddenly, those very oceans opened America to attack. Its vulnerability was clear to all on December 7. The next evening, Americans gathered around their radios to hear President Roosevelt's address to Congress. In the preceding night, he reported, Japan had attacked Hong Kong, the Philippines, Guam, and Wake Island. That morning it had attacked Midway Island. America was in a state of war. "We all sat frozen, uncomprehending, but filled with a sense of impending doom," a Nevada woman later said, capturing the mood of the nation. The war was on, and the nation was united, united in fear, but also, now, in the determination to persevere and win.

*Sea Wings to Glory,* c. 1940. Cotton (80" x 96") Parks Wildemuth Collection. *Photograph by Best Days Photography.*

Japanese Admiral Yamamoto, who had planned and commanded the operation at Pearl Harbor, was strangely quiet in the wake of its stunning success, distressed that Japan's foreign service had bungled the timing of its severance of ties with the U.S., so that the attack occurred when the two nations were still discussing peace. A sneak attack could only enrage America. As his young airmen celebrated their victory, he retired to his quarters and wrote in his journal, "I fear all we have done is to awaken a sleeping giant and fill him with a terrible resolve."

My generation were the children of that giant. Born into war, we grew up in a world charged with both tragedy and optimism. We knew the terrible costs of war, the deaths that changed our families and communities forever. On mantels and tables we saw the pictures of uniformed men who had died at places like Guadalcanal, Anzio, Tarawa, words we learned with our alphabets. But we also imbibed the absolute conviction that the political freedom that defined our national life was noble, worthy of sacrifice. Life without liberty was unthinkable. A futile war in Europe and a protracted economic depression at home had sapped America's strength, made it inward looking. It had come to doubt its vision. Pearl Harbor reawakened the nation to its historic mission, jolted it out of self-pity into purposeful, courageous action.

Throughout the Great Depression, the federal government had tried to rally the American spirit with the image of the eagle. The blue Thunderbird had been the icon of the National Recovery Administration, an agency designed, ironically, to rein in competition in business and one that was later declared unconstitutional for that reason. Fettered eagles had not worked.

Pearl Harbor lifted the fog of doubt that had obscured our vision of the heights. There, wings spread, gliding and skating on the winds of freedom, was the great bird of liberty. My generation grew up knowing the thrill of that sight and knowing we would have to keep it there for others. When the powers of human oppression put a dog in the first space satellite, we took the tough science courses that would make it possible for America to put a man on the moon, to keep space free, and the eagle visible. The children whose parents had huddled around radios on December 8, 1941, sat mesmerized before television screens on July 20, 1969, when Neil Armstrong, speaking from the surface of our moon, declared, "The eagle has landed." We were privileged to hear that, to be a part of that moment, because Pearl Harbor had awakened a sleeping giant.

*– Gaye Rice Ingram, Louisiana*

Detail, United States Navy motif in applique. Parks Wildemuth Collection. *Photograph by Best Days Photography.*

*The Eisenhower Years*, 1950 to 1959, 24" x 24", Teddy McMahon Pruett, Florida. Collection of Author. *Photograph by Best Days Photography.*

# The Eisenhower Years

Teddy does innovative work that makes an art quilt appreciator say, "Wow, what an imagination!" About her contribution to this collection, Teddy writes:

*The parameters were that the completed piece had to be 24" by 24" or less; an eagle had to figure prominently in the design; and the quilt had to be easily recognizable as depicting the 1950s. Well! I had already researched the 1950s for my Happy Daze Craze quilt, so it was a piece of cake. There are 24 fabrics in the quilt, and 23 of those are authentic 1950s fabrics. The only newer fabric is the red and white stripe, which I used as lines upon which to write phrases relating to the 1950s.*

Just look at Teddy's use of a piece of white rick rack in place of the 13 stars that usually form an arch over the eagle and makes this eagle look like she's jumping rope.

Teddy refers to her 1950s eagle as a "road-kill or flattened-out eagle." I like to call this piece brilliant.

**Quilt Technique:** Appliqué and piecing, hand quilting, and machine embellishment.

Detail, *The Eisenhower Years*, Florida. New red and white stripe fabric with 1950s phrases written in ink. Collection of Author. *Photograph by Susan Wildemuth.*

Detail, *The Eisenhower Years*, Florida. Eagle view. Collection of Author. *Photograph by Best Days Photography.*

# Teddy McMahon Pruett

Teddy McMahon Pruett, Florida. *Submitted.*

As a quilt artist and designer, Teddy McMahon Pruett says she "trashed the rulebooks." Now she makes story quilts with "recycled textiles and funky old fabrics." A gallery of her one-of-a-kind works of art can be found on her website.

As an appraiser and historian, Teddy has studied quilt and textile history for over twenty years. She received her appraisal certification in 1994, passing rigorous written and oral examinations that required her to demonstrate knowledge of three hundred years of textile history, dye process, fabric printing methods, patterns, and construction. She is also well known for her animated presentations to quilt guilds and related groups. Teddy is a member of both the American Quilt Study Group and the American Quilter's Society.

**Website:** *Teddy Pruett Quilter Appraisals and Fiber Arts.* www.teddypruett.com/

*To Everything There is a Season*, 1960 to 1969, 23" x 22", Jennifer Tenney Myers, Ohio. Collection of Author. *Photograph by Best Days Photography.*

# To Everything There is a Season

This quilt is meant to capture the spirit of the 1960s. While a violent war raged in Vietnam, the desire for peace ran through the veins of America. Yet peace seemed unattainable and the values of the 1950s irrelevant. Hippies, drugs, and communes contributed to the incoherence of the time period, which is reflected in the way I scattered the design of this quilt.

While there is a glimpse of the war itself on this quilt, I was more interested in America's reaction to the war. The design calls attention to several of the major events going on in the 1960s, including the assassinations of President John F. Kennedy and Martin Luther King, Jr., and the beginning of the American Indian Movement. The Eagle is a replica of the Apollo 11 mission patch, commemorating the history-making flight of America's first manned moon landing by Apollo 11 in 1969. As the 1962 recording of the song "Turn, Turn, Turn" by Peter Seeger observes, "To Everything There is a Season" – and the 1960s is one season that will never be forgotten.

– *Jennifer Tenney Myers*

**Quilt Technique:** Appliqué and fusing, machine appliqué, and machine quilting.

# Jennifer Tenney Myers

Detail, *To Everything There is a Season*, Ohio. Eagle view, artist's interpretation of the eagle on the Apollo 11 badge. Collection of Author. *Photograph by Best Days Photography.*

Jennifer Tenney Myers, Ohio. *Submitted.*

Jennifer Tenney Myers says:

*I have always been passionate about the arts. My mother introduced me to quilting when I was in grade school. She belonged to a small quilt group, and the members allowed me to put some stitches in the quilts on which they worked. My grandmother was a seamstress by trade and had a huge influence on me in many ways, especially in encouraging my desire to sew. Upon graduating from Ohio State University in 1998 with a degree in Music Performance (bassoon), I wanted to purchase a nice quilt. I quickly discovered I couldn't afford one. So I decided to make one. One quilt turned into two, traditional quilting turned into art quilting, and here I am over ten years later, still quilting.*

Jennifer has constructed a wide range of quilts and explored a variety of styles and techniques. She has taken classes in art quilting from David Walker and Noriko Endo and attended the Quilt/Surface Design Symposium a number of times. She says:

*When I found art quilting, my heart soared, and I have never looked back. I love the free-form nature of making an art quilt, always surprising and always drawing from creative inspiration. My inspiration comes from the world around me and from my wild stash of fabric and beads. I have won several awards over the years, including Second Place in the 2002 Sulky of America Competition in the Amateur Wearable category. My pieces have traveled with the Sulky of America Exhibit and with the Hoffman Challenge Fabric Exhibit.*

**Website:** *Jennifer's Art Quilts.* artquiltsbyjen.com/

# John F. Kennedy Assassination

## November 22, 1963

## Karen Biedler Alexander

*Mother Earth,* 39" x 34", Jennifer Tenney Myers, Ohio. Collection of Author. *Photograph by Best Days Photography.*

Karen Biedler Alexander, Washington. *Submitted. Photograph by Steve Horn Photography.*

*I was nineteen, an American living in Africa, when President John F. Kennedy was assassinated at 12:30 p.m. (C.S.T.) in Dallas, Texas on Friday, November 22, 1963.*

My father headed for Tanganyika, East Africa, in September 1962 to teach at Changombe Teacher Training College for four years under the auspices of USAID (United States Agency for International Development). Remaining stateside, my sister and I attended college for one more year while our two younger brothers completed another year of high school. Then we all dropped out of school for a year and joined our parents in Tanganyika in June 1963. (Tanganyika became Tanzania in early 1964.)

While living in East Africa, our family took a two-week camping trip across the Serengeti to Lake Victoria and back, following a circular route. That camping trip included a visit to Ngorongoro Crater, Oduvai Gorge (the archaeological site also known as "The Cradle of Mankind"), and Lake Manyara, among other places. Living in a foreign country was an amazing experience for a nineteen-year-old college student on a family sabbatical!

The shocking news about Kennedy's assassination arrived at our home in the middle of the night. Someone on a motor scooter, another American, banged on the front door, alerting our family dog whose barking woke up the entire family. My father arrived at the door right on the dog's heels and once he recognized the fellow, opened it. The messenger, who had received the first news of the assassination via short wave radio, said President Kennedy had been shot. It was only weeks earlier that I had my innocent eyes opened to the fact that governments actually participated (albeit behind the scenes) in the downfall of other governments, when Ngo Dinh Diem was assassinated in a *coup d'état* in Vietnam.

My whole family gathered in the living room to take the measure of the situation. We were stunned. At first,

All of us might wish at times
that we lived in a more tranquil world, but we don't.
And if our times are difficult and perplexing,
so are they challenging and filled with opportunity.
*– Robert F. Kennedy*

John F. Kennedy postcard. Collection of Author. *Photograph by Susan Wildemuth.*

Detail, *Mother Earth*, Ohio. Giraffe, machine thread-work, beading. Collection of Author. *Photograph by Susan Wildemuth.*

we didn't actually believe the news. I remember thinking at the time, "This only happens in Third World countries. Not in America!" Looking back, I realize our country had survived other presidential assassinations (Abraham Lincoln, James A. Garfield, and William McKinley), but at nineteen it seemed like the end of the world to me because the fall of the Diem ruling family in Saigon only weeks earlier was still fresh in my mind.

The first news we received that night mistakenly reported that Vice President Lyndon Johnson was mortally wounded, as was the Speaker of the House. I thought surely the Kennedy government was now going to fall just like the Diem government had just fallen. Having no Internet in those days and no direct access to news sources, we were in the dark for almost twenty-four hours, news trickled out of the American Embassy at a snails pace. Finally, the Embassy called in the "heads of households" of all American government personnel in the area. When our father returned from that meeting, we finally got the correct details. John Fitzgerald Kennedy, the 35th President of the United States, had been fatally wounded when shot by Lee Harvey Oswald while traveling with his wife Jacqueline, Texas governor John Connally, and his wife, Nellie Connally, in a presidential motorcade in Dallas, Texas.

I remember the day the Kennedy funeral took place. Many Catholic churches around the world held memorial masses. Although not Catholic, as a family we attended the memorial mass in Dar-es-Salaam, the capitol city of Tanganyika (Tanzania), along with almost every American and European living within driving range of the city, including diplomats from all nations that had an Embassy in Dar-es-Salaam.

*– Karen Biedler Alexander*

# 1970 to 1979

*The Quilters Evolution 1970 – 1979*, 1970 to 1979, 27" x 21.75", Kimberly Wulfert, Ph.D., California. Collection of Author. *Photograph by Best Days Photography.*

# The Quilters Evolution 1970–1979

When viewing this quilt from a distance, I hope it rings 1970s bells of recognition in quilters who began to make quilts as a hobby in that decade. Women pulled out and dusted off their mother's Singer sewing machines, on which they had learned to sew in their youth. The quilter's tools were a pair of scissors, a pencil, a twelve-inch ruler, cardboard for templates, thread, and a needle for hand-quilting the cotton and poly cotton calico, dotted Swiss, striped, or solid colored fabrics available in the period.

Detail, *The Quilters Evolution 1970 – 1979*, California. Eagle view, appliqué Collection of Author. *Photograph by Best Days Photography.*

Women used puffy polyester batting, wide binding, and square corners. The indentations in the puffy batting showed the quilting lines more than the individual stitches, which were laid either in-the-ditch or following the seam lines. Appliquéd pieces were often sewn down with zigzag or satin machine stitching; vintage patterns were hand-sewn. Few beginning quilters had perfected their skills or methods, had taken quilting classes, or knew about *Quilters Newsletter* magazine, which burst on the scene in 1969. To enhance the experience and duplicate some of the revival decade's quilts like those I had made, I put in askew measurements and stitching as part of the challenge.

**Quilt Technique:** Piecing and quilted appliqué.

As viewers get closer to the flag, they see a colonial canton and banner-waving eagle, symbol of our pledge of *E Pluribus Unum* ("out of many, one"). Founders Benjamin Franklin, Thomas Jefferson, and John Adams first suggested this motto for the Great Seal of a newly independent nation in 1776. The image also recalls a proud nation's celebration of its 200th birthday in 1976.

Drawing closer, viewers read the words that suggest the evolution of quilters in this era. Mostly women, they stepped out bravely, creatively, and passionately to establish events, businesses, research, books, fabrics, television programming, and organizations that revived quilting in this decade. From their collective vision and efforts, quilt study and quilt making acquired new esteem, developed new and vibrant forms, and created a multimillion-dollar industry for women.

In 1970, most women quilted without notice in their homes. In 1971, Jonathan Holstein and Gail Van der Hoof's display of bold geometric quilts from their collection at the Whitney Museum of Art called attention to the artistry and vibrancy of the quilting tradition in America. The Whitney exhibition created new interest in quiltmaking, extended the uses of quilts from the decorative arts to fine arts, and brought the beauty of quilts to the attention of a broader audience.

Finally, no memory of this decade would be complete without a reference to its presidents, Nixon, Ford, and Carter, and the Peace sign that symbolized a call of young people for the end of the Vietnam War.

*– Kimberly Wulfert, Ph.D.*

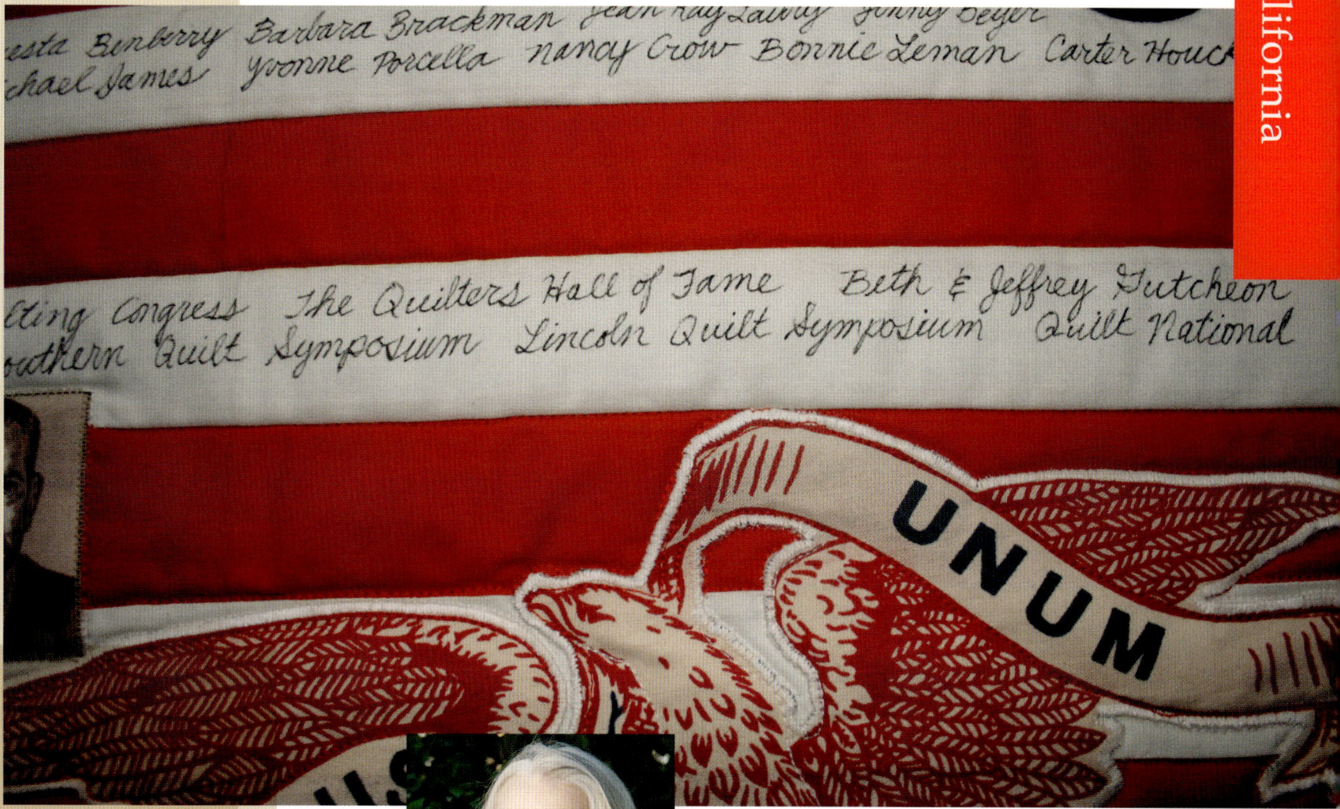


Detail, *The Quilters Evolution 1970 – 1979*, California. Significant 1970s quilt people, events, and organizations written in ink on the white lines of the flag, which show the evolution of quilters in this era. Collection of Author. *Photograph by Susan Wildemuth.*

# Kimberly Wulfert, Ph.D.

Kimberly Wulfert, Ph.D., California. *Submitted. Photography by Caitlin Jean Petersen.*

Kim describes the journey that led her to quilts and quiltmaking in the following manner. She says:

*I have been a licensed psychologist since 1989. I took my first quilt classes in 1979. My interest in antique quilts and collecting them bloomed in 1990, when I joined my first quilt guild. I took a hiatus from practicing psychology for a few years to travel the U.S. to teach, speak, lead educational tours, research, and publish on quilts and our textile history. The biography and life of John Hewson, one of the earliest chintz printers in America, was a favorite research project. Learning about the daily lives of women and the history of textile industries in France, England, India, and America in the 17th through 20th centuries captured my inquisitive mind, and I developed two Internet websites,* www.antiquequiltdating.com *and* www.antiquequiltdatingguides.com. *They have been featured in quilt magazines in Australia, England, Ireland, and the United States.*

*My research has been published in a wide array of venues in print and online, including* The Magazine Antiques, *The American Folk Art Museum's magazine* Folk Art, PieceWork, Patchwork *(France's quilt guild magazine), and American Quilt Study Group's newsletter* Blanket Statements. *For three years I wrote a column on quilt dating for* Traditional Quiltworks Magazine.

**Websites:** *New Pathways Into Quilt History.* www.antiquequiltdating.com/. *Antique Quilt Dating Guides.* www.antiquequiltdatingguides.com/
**Blog:** *Quilters Spirit.* quiltersspirit.blogspot.com/

*Moon Over Mount Eagle,* 1980 to 1989, 34.75" x 29", Georgia Bonesteel, North Carolina. Collection of Author. *Photograph by Best Days Photography.*

# Moon Over Mount Eagle

Teachers come into our lives in various ways and inspire us to become the best we can be. Georgia Bonesteel was one of those teachers who inspired me.

I was a young mom in the mid-1980s. Although I was oil painting at the time, my heart and soul really wasn't in painting, and I kept looking for something creative that would be a good fit for me. During this period I discovered Georgia Bonesteel's *Lap Quilting* and *The Victory Garden* on Saturday afternoons on our local PBS television channel, and I started taping both.

I did not have one of those grandmothers or aunts who taught me how to quilt, but the desire to learn the quilter's art lay within me. The more I watched Georgia's show, the more I thought, "I need to try this." I listened to my intuition and signed up for a hand piecing and quilting class in our local community. After the first night of class, my oil paints went into storage; I had found what I had been searching for.

**Quilt Technique:** Appliqué and Machine Piecing Quilting.

I have had three teachers who guided me on the quilting path. Jane Becker, my junior high school sewing teacher, was the first person who introduced me to sewing. Lois Ashley was my first quilting teacher at the Geneseo Community Center. And before and between the two of them, Georgia Bonesteel's books and Public Broadcasting System quilting shows encouraged me and thousands of other quiltmakers to pick up a needle and start quilting.

When deciding whom to contact for the 1980s decade, it occurred to me that it could only be one person. I chose Georgia Bonesteel to represent the decade of the 1980s because she was one of three souls who inspired me to walk down this path of quiltmaking and quilt study. I am proud to have her *Moon Over Mount Eagle* in my collection. Thanks Georgia!

– *Susan Wildemuth*

Collection of Georgia Bonesteel's *Lap Quilting* books. Collection of Author. *Photograph by Susan Wildemuth.*

# Georgia Bonesteel

Georgia Bonesteel, North Carolina. *Submitted.*

For more than thirty years, Georgia Bonesteel has been a leader in the quilt world. As the creator and host of *Lap Quilting with Georgia Bonesteel*, produced with North Carolina Public Television (UNC-TV), she has shared her enthusiasm and love of quilting on television since 1979. *Lap Quilting with Georgia Bonesteel* continues to air on PBS stations throughout the country.

A longtime seamstress, Georgia attended Iowa State University and graduated from Northwestern University. A Home Economics and Merchandizing degree enabled her to get a job in the Fashion Department of Marshall Field & Co. after college. Marriage and three children took the Bonesteels to New Orleans, where Georgia renewed her love of sewing. She became a guest on a television series, *Sewing Is Fun*, sponsored by Sears, Roebuck & Co., where she learned valuable television skills. This experience started a small business called Cajun Quilters, in which she made one-of-a-kind quilted patchwork evening bags from necktie scraps and sold them in the French Quarter.

After moving to North Carolina in 1972, she became interested in full-sized quilts and began teaching at Blue Ridge Community College in Hendersonville. Soon after that, her mother suggested she share her teaching skills on television. The rest is history.

**Website:** www.georgiabonesteel.com/
**Blog:** *Georgia Bonesteel's Blog*
www.georgiabonesteel.com/gablog.html

*Symbol of Nations,* 1990 to 1999, 23" x 24", Sharon Malec, Illinois. Collection of Author. *Photograph by Best Days Photography.*

# Symbol of Nations

The eagle has long been used as an imperial symbol. This quilt combines the traditional bald eagle as the U.S. national bird and the Native American Thunderbird eagle symbol. This piece was made with fabrics produced in the 1990s.

**Quilt Technique:** Appliqué and machine piecing and quilting.

Detail, *Symbol of Nations,* Illinois. Eagle view. Collection of Author. *Photograph by Best Days Photography.*

99

## Sharon Malec

Sharon Malec, Illinois. *Submitted.*

Sharon Malec uses a variety of hand and machine techniques to create her quilts and felted pieces. Sharon says: "As a fiber artist "I love all kinds of fabric. Fiber is a wonderfully colorful and tactile medium that produces artwork with a soft expression. I am particularly drawn to nature's colors, which complement the animal and nature subjects that dominate my work."

As a designer, Sharon is an award-winning Illinois studio quilt artist, and author. Her interest in animals and the natural world blend in her unique quilted and felted works of art.

**Website:** *Fiber art by Sharon Malec.* www.malec-designs.com/

*Baby Geniuses Eaglet*, 2000 to 2009, 15.75" x 15.75", Linda Carlson, Missouri. Collection of Author. *Photograph by Best Days Photography.*

# Baby Geniuses Eaglet

*Baby Geniuses Eaglet*, approximately 15-½ inches square, is a four-block background design that employs hand appliqué, reverse appliqué, hand quilting with metallic thread, and hand embellishments of sparkling stars and French knots. All fabrics are from Linda Carlson's fabric lines with Benartex, Inc., including "Grammie & Mimi's Baby Geniuses," "Grammie & Mimi's Baby Geniuses Grow Up," and "Grammie & Mimi's Baby Geniuses Speak Up." Linda chose to design a spread-wing baby eagle in bright and bold colors using fabrics from her collection at Benartex. She created her eaglet using hand appliqué and reverse appliqué techniques. It is a reinterpretation of *Liberty* by Dinah Jefferies.

**Quilt Technique:** Appliqué, reverse appliqué, and hand quilting.

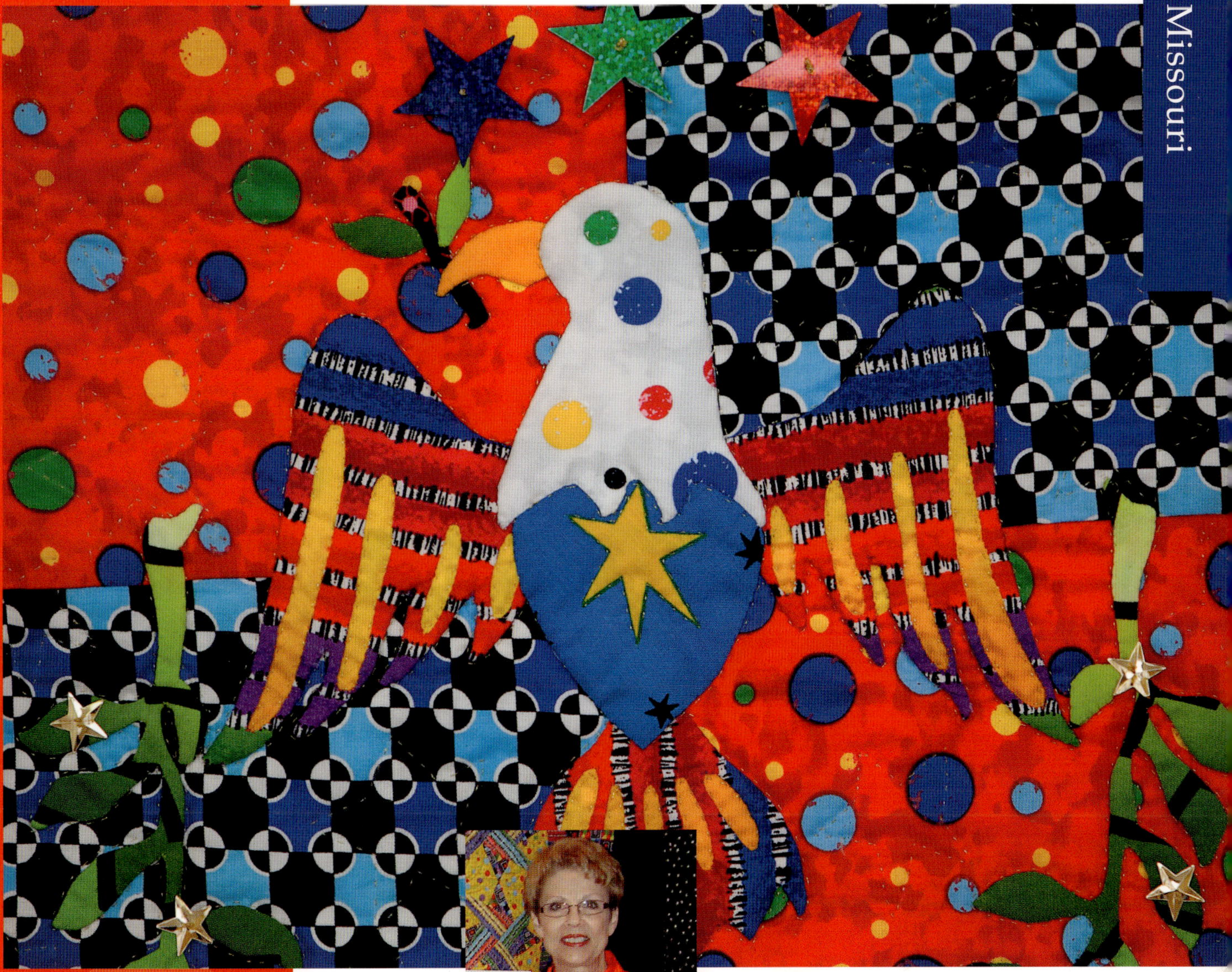

Detail, *Baby Geniuses Eaglet*, Missouri. Eagle view. Collection of Author. *Photograph by Best Days Photography.*

09

Linda Carlson, Missouri. *Submitted.*

# Linda Carlson

A University of Missouri-Columbia graduate in Elementary Education and Music Education, Linda Carlson became active in the world of quilts in the early 1980s. She is an authority on the large, four-block style of quilts and has written several books on the subject. In 2006 she and her twin sister, Diana Henage, created a fabric collection for Benartex named "Grammie & Mimi's Baby Geniuses." It was followed by "Grammie & Mimi's Baby Geniuses Grow Up." The third collection in this series, "Baby Geniuses Speak Up," premiered in 2010.

Linda teaches and lectures on hand appliqué and on four-block quilt projects ranging from large appliqué pieces to intricate *scherenschnitte* designs. Her lectures and classes include celebratory or commemorative quilts, the design of special features such as feather borders, center and corner designs, appliqué and three-dimensional techniques, and the selection of background and quilting motifs.

**Website:** *Linda Carlson Quilts.* www.lindacarlson.com/
**Blog:** *Baby Geniuses Fabric Collections.* babygeniusesfabric.blogspot.com/

# September 11, 2001

## Betty Ross

*Guardian Angel: September 11, 2001 Remembrance Quilt.* Cotton, machine pieced, machine appliquéd, and long-arm quilted (stipple quilting), 70" x 52", Mary Louise Hallenbeck, Michigan. Collection of Author. *Photograph by Best Days Photography.* Done in the style of stained glass quilts, this quilt's main feature is an eagle with "fire" in his eye. It looks like he is encircling the world in a protective embrace from an explosion.

The date September 11, 2001, rouses a mix of feelings in many Americans of sadness, anger, and fear. I was sitting at my desk at work when a co-worker called out that terrorists had flown a plane into the World Trade Center. I sat staring at my computer screen in disbelief. Terrorism was something that happened in distant foreign cities with names that were difficult to pronounce.

I thought of a close friend of mine who lived in New York City. She had been my college roommate, and I was going to ask her to be in my wedding the next summer. I could not reach her by phone, so I sent her an e-mail and waited, fear settling within the pit of my stomach.

Co-workers huddled around television screens in conference rooms. Shocking stories of other attacks were reported. A second airplane crashed into the South Tower of the World Trade Center. The Pentagon was struck. Another plane crashed in Pennsylvania.

There was a message in my Inbox from my friend in New York. At once, I was relieved that she was okay, yet horrified as I read her cryptic words, "I'm trapped. We can't get out of the city." My mind was reeling as I tried to make sense of it all. Could something of this magnitude happen in the United States? It was like something out of a science fiction novel. We could do nothing but watch the horrific events unfold, caught off-guard, shocked, and confused.

Without doubt, 9/11 demonstrated America's vulnerability. Many thought of the United States as the most powerful nation in the world, yet our leaders were powerless to prevent a coordinated terrorist attack that resulted in nearly 3,000 lives lost.

Nevertheless, rather than allowing fear to weaken and incapacitate us, we summoned our courage and pulled together as a nation. Many silent heroes selflessly put their lives at risk to save those in danger, rescue workers who perished as a result of their efforts at Ground Zero, firefighters who put the lives of those in the Twin Towers above their own lives, flight attendants on the hijacked airplanes, police officers, paramedics and those who donated money and gave blood. In the worst of times, common people, mothers, husbands, and passersby, overcame their fear and acted bravely.

In the days that followed the attacks, we were haunted by the heart-wrenching images and stories of those who lost loved ones. The healing process would take years. The New York skyline was changed forever. The way we viewed war and terrorism was changed forever. What it meant to be "safe" in this country had undeniably changed. The events of that day opened our eyes to the ever-present threat of terrorism at home.

Betty Ross, Iowa. *Submitted.*

etail, *Guardian Angel: September 11, 2001 Remembrance Quilt*, ichigan. Fire in the eagle's eye. *Photograph by Best Days Photography.*

*September 11, 2001.* Cotton, machine pieced, fused, machine quilted, beaded, 18.5" x 17", Jennifer Tenney Myers, Ohio. Collection of Author. *Photograph by Best Days Photography.* The twin towers are hand beaded with hundreds of tiny beads. The blue streaks represent the blue lights that shone in the New York sky following the disaster, and the windows and doors at the bottom of the quilt represent the debris. Both the flames and the blue lights are done by a version of reverse appliqué.

Nevertheless, our government did not hide or back down from terrorist threats. The events of 9/11 heralded change in our country. Our leaders exacted a war on terrorism. Patiently, our military forces proceeded to hunt down the man who planned the attacks and those in his organization. Airport security underwent massive changes. From the ashes emerged a new nation with heightened awareness, united in its grief, its outrage, and its new resolve.

Although years have now passed, we still feel the impact. The lessons we learned are evident in our foreign policy, our military actions, and every time we set foot in an airport, waiting in a long security line or walking through a full-body scanner. Our leaders continue their work to ensure that tragic events such as 9/11 never occur in this country again. We remember those who lost their lives that day and honor them through our actions and our resolve.

*– Betty Ross, Iowa*

*Flying Feathers*, 2010 to 2019, 24" x 19", Grace J. Errea, California. Collection of Author. *Photograph by Best Days Photography.*

# Flying Feathers

I enjoy portraiture. Animals, people, or flora close-ups, each constitutes portraiture for me. I like having the opportunity to look beyond the surface of whatever or whoever I am trying to interpret.

A few years back I was experimenting with a new machine appliqué technique, called free-edge appliqué. Unlike raw or turned-edge appliqué, in which each shape is stitched to the background around all its edges, in free-edge appliqué a shape may be only partly attached to the background. I wanted a technique that would have "free" edges to simulate a bird's feathers.

Thus, for this project, I chose to design the face of the eagle. That choice permitted me to use many feathers, each of them free-edged, and to create the texture of real feathers.

*– Grace J. Errea*

**Quilt Technique:** Machine appliqué: free-edge, machine piecing, and quilting.

Detail, *Flying Feathers*, California. Outdoor view, taken at City Park in Bettendorf, Iowa. Collection of Author. *Photograph by Best Days Photography.*

## Grace J. Errea

Grace J. Errea, California. *Submitted.*

Fiber artist, designer, and art quilter Grace J. Errea began quilting in 2000. Her art focuses on the depiction of inspiring scenes created in a contemporary, realistic manner. Grace's work has been recognized for exceptional primary use of value and secondary use of color. Her innovative techniques and depictions of nature and people have attracted widespread interest in the quilt world, as well as from national and international galleries, museums, and publications.

**Website:** *Amazing Quilts by Grace.*
www.amazingquiltsbygrace.com

*Coming Together or Falling Apart*, 2010 to 2019, 23" x 24",
Deborah Fell, Illinois. Collection of Author.
*Photograph by Best Days Photography.*

# Coming Together or Falling Apart

Reflecting on the past is easy. Predicting the future is impossible. One can dream what the future will be like, of course. I dream of peace on earth, the cure for cancer, the end of poverty and hunger, and the Cubs' winning the pennant. I see yellows to represent hope. Green is present as our earth moves toward better care of our only environment. Colors explode with hope as all the flags of the world unite. I dream of this hope, this new time of peace. What if the 2010 to 2019 decade brings us these miracles?

Then the unsettling reality of the world's state of affairs eclipses the yellows, the greens, the cures, and the peace, and a question rises in my mind: In the decade of 2010 to 2019, will the world come together or fall apart? Look at the collaged world of flags and decide for yourself. Are they coming together? Or is the world falling apart? Which way will we go? What will our world be willing to sacrifice and risk in order to become a better place? I have to believe the world will come together; I have to believe this as my children take their place as adults in an undefined world of questions.

*– Deborah Fell*

**Quilt Technique:** Painted canvas, heliographic textile paint, digital photo transfers, bamboo cotton batting, hand-dyed cotton broadcloth cotton, fiber reactive dyes, cotton thread, machine appliqué, and machine quilting.

# Deborah Fell

Detail, *Coming Together or Falling Apart,* Illinois. Eagle view, machine quilting. Collection of Author. *Photograph by Best Days Photography.*

Deborah Fell is a studio artist committed to the art quilt medium. She is a professional member of the Studio Art Quilt Associates and the Surface Design Association and has had over twenty years of education at the Quilt/Surface Design Symposium in Columbus, Ohio. Using surface treatments such as dyeing and painting fabric, Deborah focuses on abstract, organic shapes.

Detail, *Coming Together or Falling Apart,* Illinois. Full Eagle view, edge treatment, and machine quilting. Collection of Author. *Photograph by Susan Wildemuth*

Her work has been recognized nationally and has been exhibited in venues such as: the United Nations Building in New York City; the Moscone Museum in San Francisco; Art Quilt Elements at the Wayne Art Center in Philadelphia, Pennsylvania; The Works Gallery in Newark, New Jersey, a Smithsonian Institution Affiliate Museum; the U.S. Embassy in Pakistan through the U.S. State Department Arts in Embassies Program; and the premier international exhibit, "Quilt Nation." One of her art quilts appeared on the front cover of the *American Journal of Nursing*. Another is a part of the former Ground Zero Headquarters, St. Paul Trinity Chapel collection.

Deborah Fell, Illinois. *Submitted.*

In 2009, Deborah collaborated with ABC TV host Ty Pennington to create a special art project for his program *Extreme Home Makeover*, Season 7, "Montgomery House." In November of the same year, one of her art quilts was included in the Journey of Hope Exhibit in Tokyo, Japan, an exhibition that continues at the National African American Museum in Wilberforce, Ohio. Also in 2009, the artist's work was part of an exhibit sponsored by the Firelands Association for the Visual Arts in Oberlin, Ohio. Currently Deborah's work is in a traveling exhibit sponsored by the American Academy of Orthopedic Surgeons and is being exhibited in Washington, D.C. Deborah says, *"Art allows us to move from one place to the next. I create art because I believe art makes a difference in our world; it is a gift we give ourselves and it is a celebration of our souls."*

**Website:** *Deborah Fell's Art Quilts.* www.deborahfell.com

# Contact Information

Melanie Weis Bishop McCalley, Photographer
(unless otherwise noted)

Best Days Photography,
1039 State Street #206, Bettendorf, Iowa 52722
563-320-4441
**E-mail:** melanie@bestdaysphoto.com
**Website:** *Best Days Photography.* bestdaysphoto.com/

Gaye Rice Ingram, Copy Editor (Pre-Publication)
Ruston, Louisiana | **E-mail:** gingram40@gmail.com

Susan Wildemuth, Project Custodian
18621 U.S. Highway 6, Atkinson, Illinois 61235
**Website:** *Illinois Quilt History: Quilt History from the Midwest.*
www.illinoisquilthistory.com/

**Blog:** *Eye of the Needle: Quilt History Conversation from the Midwest.*
sew-eyeoftheneedlequilthistory.blogspot.com/
Susan welcomes e-mails concerning eagle quilts at
quiltingbee73@yahoo.com or wildemuthsew@gmail.com

**Special Notes:** Artist biographies, inspirations, and photos were submitted by each artist, unless otherwise noted.

# Index